THE she
GUIDE TO
BREAKING UP
& STARTING
OVER

CHRISTINA KONING

ROBSON BOOKS

First published in Great Britain in 2002 by Robson Books,
64 Brewery Road, London N7 9NT

A member of **Chrysalis** Books plc

British Library Cataloguing in Publication Data
A catalogue record for this title is available from the British
Library.

ISBN 1 86105 388 6

Typeset by FiSH Books, London WC1
Printed in Great Britain by Creative Print & Design
(Wales), Ebbw Vale

THE she GUIDE TO
BREAKING UP
& STARTING
OVER

Contents

Introduction

Marriage has never been more popular, it seems. You can't open a newspaper or a magazine these days without finding some loving twosome gazing dewily back at you. Posh and Becks, Zoe and Norman – even Tony and Cherie – all seem part of a growing trend, an unquestioning affirmation of the joys of coupledom. All the world loves a lover, and it would be downright mean to grudge these lovers their happiness, and the social rituals – weddings, anniversaries, Valentine's Day – that go with it. But, for anyone going through the infinitely more painful and difficult rites of passage surrounding divorce and separation, these constant reminders of other people's relationship successes can feel like salt rubbed in a wound. It looks as if everyone else has achieved a happy-ever-after ending to their particular fairy tale – except you.

Yet, despite the enduring popularity of matrimony, increasing numbers of us are getting divorced, apparently. In fact, Britain has the second highest divorce rate in Europe; only Denmark is higher. A recent survey conducted by the Family Policy Studies Centre found that two out of every five marriages in Britain end in divorce, with the figure even higher for cohabiting couples. Twenty-eight per cent of children now under sixteen will experience their parents' separation. More than 40 per cent of all marriages are remarriages. The average length of marriage that ends in divorce is ten years, but one-third of all divorces take place within the first five years. Maybe, after all, the notion that marriage is for keeps is one that needs updating. Far from being a society of couples tied together for life, we have become one in which single people are in a growing (and vocal) minority, and in which marriage is now regarded as merely one option out of many.

The poor princess would have to find out what life was all about.

This isn't all bad news of course. The days when unhappy couples stayed together 'for the sake of the children' are thankfully gone. Nor is there the kind of stigma attached to divorce that once existed – it has become far too widespread for that. The very public separations of Prince Charles and Diana Spencer, Princess Anne and Mark Phillips, and Prince Andrew and Sarah Ferguson have shown that even the royal family is not exempt from this particular social trend. And – despite all the column inches devoted to celebrity weddings – you have only to open a newspaper to see the other side of the story, with at least as many column inches devoted to recent high-profile break-ups such as those of Mick Jagger and Jerry Hall, Patsy Kensit and Liam Gallagher, Meg Matthews and Noel Gallagher, Mel B and Jimmy Gulzar or Meg Ryan and Dennis Quaid, as to celebrity weddings and christenings. Not only are people getting divorced more than they did in the past – they're also talking about it more!

Which was one of the reasons I wanted to write this book. Because – despite this new climate of openness – divorce remains one of the most painful rites of passage anyone can go through, as disruptive and upsetting, in its way, as bereavement. However much nonsense is talked about the 'frivolousness' with which people nowadays allegedly enter into marriage, or decide to get divorced, the fact remains that no one makes this kind of decision lightly. It can be a long and painful process, involving not only the two separating partners, but at least two families. It is never easy at a psychological level, even if the legal side of it has been simplified in recent years.

But, while no one would deny that getting divorced can be horrible, it's important to remember that it isn't the end of everything. What seems, at the time, like a wholly negative and destructive thing can actually be the start of something new. There are many reasons why relationships end; some of them will be examined in this book. What is certain is that the ending of one relationship isn't a reason to give up on your whole life – in fact, it can be an opportunity to transform your life into something better, stronger and more fulfilling.

1
Breaking Up is Hard to Do

Once upon a time there was a beautiful princess. She had golden hair, blue eyes and a kind heart, and one day a prince came along and asked her to marry him. She said yes at once, because she had always wanted to get married, and because she loved children and hoped to have some of her own. The wedding was a splendid occasion, and the whole country turned out to see the princess in her magnificent white gown and lace veil, being married to her handsome prince. 'A fairytale wedding,' everyone said – which was exactly what it was. In due course, the princess gave birth to a son, and for a time it seemed as if her happiness must be complete. But then, not long after the birth of her second son, the princess realised that the prince didn't love her any more, and that made her very unhappy. But what could she do? Fairytale princesses don't get divorced. They're supposed to live happily ever after. Suddenly, it looked as if the poor princess would have to find out what real life was all about...

It's an all-too-familiar story (and not just because of the obvious similarity to our own royal fairy-tale-gone-wrong). Even in this day and age, the romantic ideals live on. Most people want to get married. Most think they'll find their 'heart's desire' in another person. A surprising number believe that, having found that person, their feelings of love and respect towards them will never change. This is despite worsening divorce statistics, increasingly permissive attitudes towards casual sex and the fact that people now live longer, so that 'till death us do part' has become a far more serious commitment (in terms of time at least) than it ever was before. What is perhaps most surprising is how many women of the mid-to-late-twenties generation – women who have grown up in the postfeminist era, and who take for granted notions of gender equality and the right to work that their mothers' generation fought for – still cherish the same romantic dreams about getting married as, well, their grandmothers did. Women who wouldn't dream of not paying their half of the bill, or who'd think themselves patronised by any man who dared to offer them his seat on the tube, come over all gooey at the thought of white lace and tulle, and spend hours window-shopping for the perfect engagement ring.

'I wanted it all – no question,' says Kate, who at 28 was already running her own software business, when she and her boyfriend decided to make it 'legal'. 'The big wedding: white dress, Rolls-Royce – the lot. Even though Sean and I had been living together for four years, I still felt I wanted it to be a big deal. I'm an only child, so my parents really pushed the boat out. I got married from my parents' home, in Suffolk, so we took over a small local hotel to put up the guests who'd come up from London, and we'd invited *everybody*. I felt quite guilty afterwards, because it must have cost a fortune – and my parents aren't particularly well off – but at the time, it seemed like the only way to do it. Now, of course, I wish we'd saved the money.'

Kate and Sean had discussed having children 'in a year or two', but it wasn't something they'd given much thought to when planning their Big Day. 'Most of my friends were at the age where they were starting to have babies, and I knew it was an option eventually,' says Kate, whose first child, Liam, arrived barely a year after the wedding. 'But I don't think I realised how hard it would hit us – the whole baby thing. From having been a couple, with a brilliant social life and a fairly high disposable income between us, we became a family – with all that that implies, in terms of diminished income. Suddenly, every decision was focused around Liam and his needs. Instead of spending our money on things for us – holidays, a new car – we were spending it on the baby. And our sex life suffered, because I was so knackered all the time. I don't think either of us was prepared for how much difference having a child makes to the relationship.'

Then Sean lost his job as a result of management restructuring at the publishing firm where he worked. It was ten months before he found another job – during which time the tensions in the marriage worsened. Kate, who was trying to combine running her business from home with bringing up an active toddler, felt that too much of the burden had been placed on her shoulders at once. 'I got really resentful towards Sean, because I felt in some way he'd let me down, by not keeping to his side of the bargain. Here I was, three years into a marriage which was supposed to be an equal partnership, having to deal with all the financial side – paying the mortgage on the flat and everything else – as well as trying to be a mother to Liam. It all got too much.'

Even when Sean did manage to get a job, the couple found it hard to get back on their feet again.

'We'd built up so much debt, that it was a struggle just trying to pay it off. And I'd been losing clients, because I couldn't afford to pay someone to help me develop the business. So in fact it was almost worse when Sean found a job, because I lost out on the childcare side.'

In the end, the relationship got so strained that Sean moved out. The couple tried relationship counselling, through Relate, but Kate now feels they left it too late before seeking help. 'Basically, we'd had so many awful rows about money that neither of us felt we could go back to trusting the other. I felt I'd been let down by Sean – emotionally and financially – when I needed him most, and he felt I wasn't the same fun-to-be-with person he'd fallen in love with.'

Kate and Sean's story is one that has become all too typical in recent years: a successful, professional couple, who've apparently 'got it all' – good jobs, nice flat, a relatively high income – discover that having a child early on in the marriage puts an untenable strain on a previously carefree relationship. Sometimes, this can be because one member of the partnership isn't ready to surrender his or her bachelor 'freedom', and finds the relentless demands of financing a mortgage, or providing for a baby, more than he or she can cope with. In many cases, these feelings of resentment or anxiety about commitment disappear after a short while, to be replaced by new feelings of maturity and responsibility. Occasionally – as in Kate and Sean's case – the initial tensions of adjusting to married life are exacerbated by the added pressure of serious financial problems. Getting married and having a baby are joyful – but also highly stressful – occasions. If one considers that many couples not only put themselves through both in the space of a few months, but also frequently choose to move house during the same period, it's hardly surprising some of them end up feeling the strain.

For some couples, the problems arise because one or other decides they don't want children – while their partner does. With many couples choosing to delay parenthood until both are well into their thirties, this kind of conflict often doesn't become apparent for the first few years of the marriage, as both partners focus on pursuing career goals. Often, it's only when friends start having children that the pressure becomes intense. Couples who've previously enjoyed all the benefits of having a double income, and a 'singles' lifestyle, are suddenly faced with the possibility of making a major life change that will radically alter not only their financial arrangements, but also the balance of their emotional life.

'Everything was fine until I hit my thirties,' says Louise, now a senior registrar at a big London hospital. 'John and I were both so busy working – we met when we were both junior doctors – that we never gave a thought to having kids. Everyone else we knew was working like crazy, too; at weekends one of us was always "on call". Somehow, we managed to fit in a pretty active social life as well – apart from the usual dinner parties and going out to restaurants, we used to spend every holiday doing something exotic. John loves travelling, so it was India one year, Australia the next. We were both earning quite good salaries by this time, so we could afford to do all this and still buy the house we wanted, in one of the nicer areas of north London. I remember thinking when we first went to look at the place – which needed a lot of doing up, but was basically a lovely, family house – that this would be a good place to bring up kids. John didn't see it like that, of course.'

Louise had reached a stage in her career when she could have chosen to take maternity leave, without damaging her promotion prospects too much. She knew it meant that John would be taking on the main financial responsibility for a few months, but thought he'd be happy to do so. Other thirtysomething couples they knew were 'downshifting' to have children; Louise saw no reason why she and John shouldn't do the same. 'Having kids wasn't at the top of the agenda for either of us when we first got married, but, as time went on, I started to want it more and more.' Unfortunately, she hadn't realised how attached John was to the life they'd built up together. 'John was devastated when I told him I wanted a child. He said he just wasn't ready (at thirty-two!) to take on the responsibility of caring for another human being. He got really upset with me. He seemed to think I was only giving in to the idea because of peer-group pressure – as if having a baby was like acquiring a new designer accessory – but I knew it meant much more to me than that. It was then that I found myself taking a long, hard look at what the relationship had become, and realising that perhaps we weren't as well suited as I'd always thought. John's reluctance to have children wasn't the only reason we broke up – but it was probably the single most important reason.'

These couples, and thousands like them, have found their relationships tested – often, sadly, to breaking point – by the all-important question of having children. There's a certain inevitability to this, of course. Having a baby is the moment in a relationship when two become three – the moment when all you thought you knew about the other person has to be reconsidered, in the light of your new roles as parents. Suddenly, the fun-loving guy you married, who used to think nothing of going clubbing till the small hours, turns into a gloomy grouch, who won't even get up to help with the baby's feeds, while the girl *he* thought he'd promised to love for ever has metamorphosed into a whining harridan, smelling of regurgitated milk, instead of Chanel Number 5. Sleepless nights, rows about money and the secret anxieties that most new parents have, of not 'measuring up' to some imagined ideal of parenthood can all place a strain on a relationship.

'I felt Rachel had become this completely different person,' says Tim, a teacher at an inner-city comprehensive, now in his late thirties. 'She'd always been so sure of herself and independent – not a clinging, feminine type at all. It was what I loved about her. But, when Poppy was born, she got terribly stressed about everything. I'd come home from work to find her in floods of tears because the house was looking a bit messy. She was always complaining that I didn't do my share. When I did try to help – with bathing Poppy or changing her – she'd say I wasn't doing it right. She was a very nervous mother. It got so that, if I came across one of those articles about cot death or childhood allergies in the paper, I used to hide it from her. She was incredibly protective of Poppy – almost obsessively so. The thing is, Rachel's an only child, whereas I'm the eldest of four. I was used to having my younger brother and sisters around when I was growing up. I think Rachel was a bit scared by the whole idea of looking after a baby.'

Things didn't improve when the couple's second child, Jack,

was born. Rachel (who'd gone back to work for a brief period
when Poppy started nursery school) decided to quit her teaching
job, and devote herself to full-time motherhood. This seemed
initially like a good idea: Tim had recently been promoted to
deputy head, and the loss of their second income, Rachel said,
would be offset by their not having to pay a childminder.
However, the decision was to have disastrous consequences for
the marriage. 'I felt that Rachel excluded me from the early years
of the children's childhood,' says Tim. 'It was as if she resented
the fact that I still had a career, while she didn't, and wanted to
make me feel bad about not spending more time with the family.
I'd get home from work after a gruelling day and the first thing
she'd say was how exhausted she was from looking after the kids.
It caused a lot of rows.'

When Tim started having an affair with a colleague at work,
the relationship between him and Rachel deteriorated further.
Resenting the fact that he was always 'working late', Rachel
accused him of taking her for granted. Overwhelmed by guilt,
Tim decided to end the affair, in order to try to make his marriage
work. But a chance remark by a friend aroused Rachel's
suspicions, and when she confronted Tim he confessed that he
had been unfaithful. 'It was almost as if she was pleased to have
a real reason for all her anger,' says Tim. 'It was as if, all those
years, she'd been pushing me away – and, when I finally lived up
to her view of me as a selfish bastard, she felt vindicated.'

Infidelity is often seen as a 'cause' of divorce and separation,
whereas in fact it is a symptom. Couples who enjoy a successful
relationship don't, as a rule, feel the compulsion to stray that is so
often experienced by those whose relationships are under stress.
Boredom is sometimes given as the reason why married couples
'play away' – but, while it is certainly true that a clandestine
affair can spice up a failing marriage, it can also be terribly
destructive. All close relationships are based on trust, and, once
that is gone, a marriage can seem a grotesque charade. Telling lies

to someone you are supposed to care about is demeaning, both for the person telling the lies and for the one being lied to. It's often this – rather than the actual infidelity itself – that a betrayed partner finds hardest to forgive.

'I felt as if I couldn't trust Paul ever again,' says Gemma, aged 34, who runs her own successful PR company. 'Knowing he'd lied to me for two years about his affair was just incredibly hurtful. It made me reassess our whole relationship – because, if he could lie about that, maybe he'd been lying all along when he said he cared about me.' Paul, whose job in advertising often took him abroad for meetings and conferences, had seemed increasingly distant towards her, Gemma now realises. 'I put it down to work tensions – advertising's a very competitive field – but, with hindsight, I can see it went deeper than that. We used to argue about pointless things – what restaurant to go to, that kind of thing – and it seemed as if Paul was always criticising me. One day, he was talking about this girl he knew at work, and it was "Sara this" and "Sara that", and I suddenly twigged, and said to him, "You're sleeping with her, aren't you?" He denied it at first, but later he admitted he was. What was really horrible was that I realised it must have started when I was pregnant with Ellie.'

Gemma insisted on a trial separation, during which time Paul moved in with his girlfriend, Sara. This relationship ended after a few months – partly, Gemma thinks, because Paul felt so unhappy being apart from her and their two children – and Paul asked if he could come back. 'We tried it for a while,' says Gemma. 'But it was a nonstarter. Paul was just so miserable all the time, brooding about the break-up with Sara, and I felt very angry towards him for what he'd done to our marriage. I'd only agreed to give it another chance because of the children. But when we started arguing again, I just thought, Sod this. I told Paul I wanted a divorce.' Although she had misgivings about ending the marriage, she now feels it was the only thing to do. 'Our relationship was dead. It seemed ridiculous to be carrying on as if everything could just go back to the way it had been. Six years on, I think it was the right decision for both of us.'

Even in these divorce-prone days, couples do still try to 'make a go of it' – sometimes for religious reasons, as well as 'for the sake of the kids'. Where both partners have been unfaithful, it is often, paradoxically, easier to patch things up again, perhaps because neither person feels more betrayed than the other. The controversial 'open marriages' that hit the headlines during the Swinging Sixties worked for this reason, presumably. But, where one partner in a relationship feels that he or she has been duped by the other, the feelings of sexual and emotional betrayal can be hard to forgive. 'I knew Richard was having affairs, but I chose to turn a blind eye while the children were small,' says Teresa, an artist, now in her early forties, whose husband is an academic. 'I used to tell myself he'd "grow out of it", and that I was the only important one in his life. The funny thing was, I think he really did care about me, in his own way. I always knew when he was seeing another woman, because he would be terribly nice to me, and buy me presents – which he never did normally.'

As a Catholic, Teresa initially resisted the idea of getting a divorce. She also didn't want to disrupt family life for her three children, now in their teens. 'I suppose I rather naïvely thought that Richard would always be around, even though we had no sex life to speak of, and were both leading separate lives. Then I met somebody else. It was so liberating, after all those years of being taken for granted, to find out what I'd been missing. I remember how shocked Richard was when he found out about it. I suppose he'd assumed I'd be around for ever, too.'

The couple are not yet divorced, but now live separately, which Teresa feels is a much better arrangement. 'We're actually quite good friends, now. I think it was an eye-opener for Richard, finding out that I wasn't going to play his game any more. And of course it's been good for me, having Josh around the place. The kids are surprisingly relaxed about it all.'

As will be apparent from the case histories discussed above (in all of which, needless to say, names and minor details have been changed), breaking up can occur for a wide range of reasons. Financial problems, disagreements about whether to have children, the stress of being a new parent, the shock of finding out about infidelity – all can be contributory factors. Added to which are other causes, less easy to identify, but no less crucial, when it comes to understanding why a relationship has broken down. Perhaps the most obvious of these is lack of compatibility. With so many couples living together before marriage, it seems surprising that there are still people who decide to commit themselves to another person on a long-term basis without knowing very much about them. Fundamental things – such as whether two people laugh at the same things, or have the same priorities in life – are frequently disregarded when a wedding is being planned. The powerful sexual attraction couples often feel at the beginning of a relationship can often obscure more down-to-earth questions such as 'Do I really like this person?' and 'Does he/she think the same way as I do about things that are important to me?' Even apparently trivial matters – such as whether your spouse is a slob or a tidiness fanatic, or whether he/she prefers to spend his/her free time curled up on the sofa with a good book, or going white-water rafting – can make or break a marriage in its early stages.

Deciding to separate

The decision to separate from your partner is not one you will undertake lightly, but, even so, it makes sense to be absolutely clear that this is what you want to do. If your partner has left you for another person, or if there are irreconcilable differences that make it impossible for the two of you to live together, then you may already have decided that parting is the only course of action.

For many couples, however, things are not so clear-cut. When a relationship is breaking down, it can take months of doubt and confusion before one or both partners make the decision to end the relationship. So take the time to ask yourself, Is this really what I want? (Don't worry about the children – if you have them – at this stage. You have to be clear in your own mind.)

Make a list of your partner's good points

Does he/she

- attract you?
- show you tenderness?
- look after you?
- behave to you as a good friend?
- make you laugh?

Now make a list of your partner's bad points

Does he/she

- bore you?
- treat you unkindly?
- behave inconsiderately?
- show no interest in you?
- act irresponsibly towards you?

Compare the two lists, and consider whether the good points outweigh the bad points, or vice versa. If it is the latter, then ask yourself, Why am I still with this person, who treats me so inconsiderately? Do I still love them, in spite of their bad behaviour? Is it worth seeking counselling or mediation, in order to save the relationship? This may seem like an obvious exercise to do, but it is surprising how many people do not actually seem to *know* why they are separating from their partner. One of the most common answers to the question 'Why are you getting divorced?' is 'Because we've both changed.' But people do not necessarily have to grow apart when they change.

Of course, no relationship is perfect, and even the most enduring marriages occasionally go through difficult patches. Discovering what makes your partner 'tick' and learning how to give and take are all part of the learning process most of us have to go through – and, indeed, a relationship can actually be strengthened through this process. But, when couples fall out, what once seemed unimportant can assume enormous significance. Suddenly, the fact that he once forgot her birthday or that she has a tendency to splurge on payday becomes symbolic of everything that is wrong with the relationship. 'You've never cared about me!' she'll say, and he'll counter by saying, 'You're so extravagant.' When two people are on the verge of breaking up, everything they do or say gets added to the long list of grievances. All of a sudden, the fairy tale is over, and there's nothing left but the cold, harsh light of day.

For many couples, these warning signs are ignored for too long, and the relationship is irreparably damaged. Others decide to seek counselling, as a way of bringing such divisions out in the open, and then working through them. This can be very effective, although, as one former Relate counsellor told me, 'Many people don't seek help until it is really too late. There's a tendency to assume that counsellors will automatically advise people to stay together at all costs, whereas, in fact, we're often helping them to arrive at a very different conclusion. What we're offering is a kind of safe area, within which people can discuss their problems, and perhaps decide on an amicable separation, if that's what's best for them.'

For anyone who hasn't been through a major break-up, it can sometimes be hard to understand exactly what's going on when two people who've lived together in apparent harmony suddenly decide to part. 'What went wrong?' is a question you get asked a lot – and one that, of course, you and your partner might also be asking yourselves. After my own separation, I found one of the most difficult things was convincing others – family and friends

– that my husband and I were serious about our decision to split. 'But you always seemed so perfect together,' was one friend's comment, while another actually burst into tears, and cried, 'I don't believe it!'

The sad truth is, that by the time you and your partner have made the decision to 'go public', you'll both be pretty sure that the decision to divorce is the right one. You will have been through all the reasons why you 'ought' to stay together (the children, your parents, your jobs) and will have come to the conclusion that, important as these and other considerations are, they are not, in the end, enough to keep the two of you together for the rest of your lives. You will have discussed the financial implications – who pays the mortgage and what about the children's school fees? – and have arrived at some kind of (at least temporary) agreement. You will have had tearful conversations and sleepless nights.

Because, make no mistake, what you are both about to go through isn't easy. There'll be times you'll wish everything could just go back to being the way it used to be. But the important thing to remember is that being in an unhappy relationship isn't a life sentence. The days when 'wedlock' was synonymous with 'deadlock' are thankfully a thing of the past.

2
Where Did We Go Wrong?

When a relationship breaks down, it is only natural to want to blame the other partner for his or her failure to live up to the expectations you might have had. It becomes convenient to shove all the responsibility for what went wrong in the marriage onto just one person – whereas, in reality, things are seldom that clear-cut. 'It takes two to make a quarrel', as the saying goes. Indeed, blaming your partner solely for the break-up can actually delay your recovery from it. Instead of coming to terms with the fact that the two of you now want different things, and may in fact be happier apart, you waste energy on pointless recrimination. Equally damaging is the effect this can have on any children of the relationship (an aspect discussed more fully in Chapter 4) – so it makes sense to make the break in as considered a way as possible. Storming out of the house at three o' clock in the morning is the sort of thing divorcing couples do in bad movies. Of course, sometimes life is *like* a bad movie – but, if you have a choice, try to minimise the histrionic scenes.

The decision to part can be sudden and explosive – such as when one partner discovers that the other has been unfaithful – or it can be a slow process, arrived at after weeks or even months of discussion. Even if your separation is of the former kind, it can make sense to spend some time talking things over with your partner, before you decide to involve the outside world. Once other people – children and other family members – are in the know, it can be hard to sort out the 'public' version of what happened from the private version, which concerns only the two of you. Taking the time, where possible, to discover 'what went wrong' can be beneficial – if only because, in identifying the causes of estrangement, it can help both of you to avoid making the same mistakes in the future.

Being willing to listen to your partner's account of how, in his or her view, the relationship has failed is not a sign of weakness, but of 'taking charge' of events. Even if you are very angry with your partner, it can help to try to take an objective view of matters. If you are going to separate, there will be many practicalities to sort out, which will involve careful negotiation. It can often help to clear the air if you talk about how you both feel about the relationship, before embarking on the more down-to-earth stuff. However, you shouldn't just launch into this – it has to be carefully planned. Telling your partner how angry and upset you are, without any preliminary build-up, can deteriorate very quickly into a row – exactly what you don't want to happen!

Avoid 'bad' times when trying to discuss what went wrong.

So try to fix a time that suits you both – after the children are in bed, for example. Avoid 'bad' times, such as when you have both just come in from work, or when you have friends over. This may seem an obvious thing to say, but it is surprising how many people do embark on this kind of conversation when they have a captive audience of embarrassed outsiders. Remember: you're not setting out to have a quarrel with your partner, but to try to understand what went wrong in your marriage. This is both so that you can remain on as good terms with your spouse as possible while you are going through the difficult and painful process of divorce, and so that you will be able to avoid going through anything of the kind again. Of course it makes sense to have some ground rules.

- **Rule 1: This is not an argument.** If either or both of you get upset, or start to shout or become abusive, then the discussion will stop.
- **Rule 2: Each person should talk about his or her own feelings, not criticise the other.** Your aim is to help your partner understand how you feel, and to try to understand how your partner feels – not to score points.
- **Rule 3: Both partners should have equal time to talk.** Agree on a time limit of, say, half an hour for the whole discussion. Divide the time equally. You talk for fifteen minutes, then your partner talks (or vice versa). Agree that there should be no interruptions.
- **Rule 4: The one listening should give his or her full attention.** While one of you speaks, the other should listen without trying to interrupt or comment.

When it is your turn to talk, try to explain how you feel as clearly and objectively as possible, without raising your voice or giving in to emotional outbursts. For example, if your partner has hurt you by having an affair with someone else, just say how rejected and unhappy this makes you feel. Don't resort to name-calling, and don't drag the 'other person' (i.e. your partner's lover) into it. This is about you and your partner, not some third party.

When it is your partner's turn to talk, try to listen to what he or she is telling you. If the cause of the break-up is infidelity, there may be a reason for this, other than the obvious one of sexual gratification. Most people don't have affairs unless something else in the marriage is wrong. This may be your chance to find out what has been making your partner unhappy. Even if you feel that he or she is resorting to 'special pleading', resist the urge to comment.

After this conversation you will both need time to consider what the other person has said. If the discussion has gone well, you may feel the need to talk about things some more – using the same ground rules. By this time, you may be able to move on to the next stage in your negotiations. If you have both decided to separate, you need to discuss the whys and wherefores of this. How are you going to break it to the children? Is one of you going to move out of the family home? Conversely, you may feel that you need to seek professional advice. Some couples who have taken the time to talk discover that, after all, they may not be ready to separate. If this is the case with you and your partner, you need to contact a professional counselling service, such as Relate. Here, the discussion between the two of you about the future of your marriage will be 'refereed' by a trained counsellor.

If, on the other hand, your initial discussion with your partner indicates that you have both reached the end of the road in your relationship, then it is as well to take stock of the situation and decide how best to proceed. When you have arrived at this point, it can sometimes be helpful to lay out a personal set of ground rules, to guide you through the difficult times ahead. The main point to bear in mind is what *you* want from the future. Do you want to separate from your partner in as amicable a way as possible, so that the two of you can remain on cordial terms? Do you want to be happy in the future with another person, without repeating the mistakes you may have made in your present relationship? If the answer to these two questions is yes, then you need to look long and hard at your feelings towards your partner, and at your own priorities. As with most things in life, there is a negative and a positive way of doing this.

Negative: You want your partner to suffer. If you have been hurt, then feelings of revenge are only natural. However, you should try to curb these feelings, if you can. Most of us know the saying that 'love is the nearest thing to hate', and this can all too often be the case when a relationship has gone sour. People who try to punish their exes by making their lives a misery are in reality just trying to keep the relationship going. As long as you are driven by feelings of anger towards your partner, you are not free to establish a good relationship with anyone else.

Positive: You want to stop suffering yourself. The way to do this is to focus on *your* needs, and *your* future – not those of your partner. If you need to think in terms of revenge, remember the saying, 'Living well is the best revenge'. It is a tried-and-tested formula, but it really does work! If your marriage has ended, you need to think in terms of what lies ahead – not constantly be harking back to the past. Having talked over with your partner the reasons why your marriage has failed, and perhaps tried to work through those grievances with a counsellor, you need to look to the future – *your* future. If you can get to the point, some way down the line, when you can think of your ex with sympathy and understanding rather than hatred or resentment, then you will have achieved a great deal.

Negative: You want to prove your partner was in the wrong. This, again, is all part of the destructive cycle of blame many couples go through when a marriage ends. Saying 'It was all *your* fault!' is so much easier than admitting that there may have been faults on both sides and that neither of you is more to blame than the other. If this sounds hard, then think about it: you married your partner, didn't you? You must have been able to see his or her point of view at that time. By demonising your ex, you are doing neither of you any favours – just prolonging the agony of break-up.

Positive: You are willing to admit your own mistakes. When you can see that there was fault on both sides – because no relationship is ever that clear-cut – then you will have taken an important step towards recovering your own sense of self-worth and, ultimately, achieving happiness in the future. Taking your share of responsibility for 'what went wrong' is an essential part of being in control of the situation. You're not a passive victim, but someone who's in charge of his or her own life. Even if you were not the main instigator of the break-up, you need to look hard at what part your actions (or inactions) played in the eventual outcome. This might hurt (the truth is seldom comfortable), but it will be worth it if it leaves you free of bitterness towards your partner.

Negative: You want the children to be on your side. One of the worst side effects of an acrimonious divorce is the effect it has on the warring couple's children. If you try to turn your children against the other parent, you are risking their future happiness, and making it much harder for them to handle the divorce itself. It may be a hard pill to swallow, but remember: *your partner has a right to a good relationship with your children, too*. Whatever the rights or wrongs of the case, you owe it to them to keep this in mind.

Positive: You want your children to come out of the break-up undamaged. Putting your children's wellbeing higher than your own resentful feelings towards your partner is always the best option (see Chapter 4 for further discussion of this approach). Even if your partner has behaved badly towards you, you should not let this colour your attitude towards him/her as far as your children are concerned. Children need to be allowed to love both their parents, in order to develop into well-balanced adults who can form loving relationships of their own. As they grow up, they will start to understand more about the role each of their parents has played in their upbringing. If you have been generous towards your partner, and attempted to heal the rift between you, your children will eventually come to appreciate this.

Negative: You want to get as much as you can from the marriage, in terms of property. Dividing up the home and other financial assets can often be a highly emotional process (see Chapter 7 for further discussion of this). Sometimes the struggle for assets becomes a substitute for a different kind of struggle. When you make an issue of 'who gets what', you risk turning the separation process into a battle – resulting in further bitterness between you and your ex.

Positive: You want a fair settlement. If your intention when dividing up the property you and your ex have shared is to be as fair as possible, you make it possible for both of you to show generosity in the future. By refusing to let financial matters and property become a battleground, you will have won the most important battle – the one with yourself. If you can feel you've behaved as well as possible, it will be easier for you to come to terms with what has happened. Your ex will be more willing to negotiate with you over other matters (such as the children's welfare). You may find you end up getting a good deal – without having to fight for it.

All these and other aspects of the break-up process are covered in more detail later. What I want to establish here is how important it is to get a perspective on what you want from life *after* divorce. Do you really want to stay 'married' to your ex for ever? Or do you want to make a fresh start, with the chance of happiness in the future? No contest, really – is it?

3
Getting the Right Legal Advice

How do I start divorce proceedings?

For many people, the most daunting thing about getting divorced is the idea of the legal process itself, with its prospect of long, drawn-out legal battles over property and visiting rights, and its threat of huge legal bills at the end. But, until we have to go through this ourselves, most of us have no idea what's involved

It's not surprising that many of us dread the prospect of having to go through with what could turn into a lengthy – and expensive – battle of wills.

– nor how to cope with the nitty-gritty of the procedure. Horrible phrases such as 'his ex really took him to the cleaner's' or 'since the divorce, she's really had to struggle' sum up what most of us fear might happen to us, if we were ever to find ourselves in the divorce courts. When horrible imaginings become reality, it's not surprising that many of us dread the prospect of having to go through with what could turn into a lengthy – and expensive – battle of wills.

Of course it doesn't have to be like that. Nowadays, many solicitors are well versed in conciliation techniques, which are intended to reduce antagonism between a divorcing couple, not inflame it. And for those couples who are not fundamentally in disagreement over major issues, such as visiting rights, there are cheaper, 'do-it-yourself' options. Some people even get by without retaining a lawyer – although there may be the need for consultation at some stage in the procedure, just in order to be able to avoid the inevitable confusions that can arise when trying to negotiate a settlement. Just think of all the red tape involved in selling a house, for example (although, increasingly, many people are choosing to do *that* themselves).

So what exactly is involved in getting a divorce, and how can you minimise the stress for you and your family?

Well, first of all you can rest assured that, if you are retaining a solicitor to represent you, then he or she will handle most of the paperwork for you. But, as with any legal procedure, it is as well to be aware of what is involved at each stage, in order to keep abreast of what is happening – and to keep costs down! Never be afraid to ask your solicitor if there is anything you do not understand about any stage of the process. This is part of your solicitor's job – to make sure that you are in the picture about your divorce and its probable outcomes for you and your children.

If, however, you have chosen not to retain a solicitor, then you can get hold of the information you need from the court where your petition is going to be heard. Here, you can pick up the following leaflets, all of which have been written with clarity and plain speaking in mind (so much so that they have been awarded the 'Crystal Mark' by the Plain English Campaign):

Leaflet 1: About divorce
Leaflet 2: I want to get a divorce – what do I do?
Leaflet 3: Children and divorce
Leaflet 4: The respondent has replied to my petition – what do I do?
Leaflet 5: I have a decree nisi – what must I do next?

These leaflets will explain how to fill in the necessary forms that are involved in each stage of the divorce process. The first of these is the **form of petition**. This requires details of you and your spouse, including: names, addresses, occupations and the names and dates of birth of any children of the marriage. In addition, the petition will detail which of the five circumstances – called **grounds for divorce** – is being used to show that the marriage has irretrievably broken down. These are as follows:

1. One spouse has committed adultery. In addition, the petitioner must state that, as a result of the adultery, he or she finds it intolerable to go on living with the adulterous spouse (except Northern Ireland)
2. One spouse has behaved unreasonably. The law defines this as: 'the respondent has behaved in such a way that the petitioner cannot reasonably be expected to live with the respondent.' Examples of unreasonable behaviour include violence, excessive drinking, excessive gambling or other financial irresponsibility, and a refusal to have sex.
3. One spouse has deserted the other for a period of at least two years. To 'desert' means simply to leave against the wishes of the remaining spouse.
4. The husband and wife have been separated for at least two

years and both spouses consent to divorce.
5. The husband and wife have been separated for at least five years. In this case, the consent of the respondent is not required.

Who is the respondent?
The spouse who is not the petitioner. It is up to the spouse to *respond* to the petition.

Who is the co-respondent?
In petitions in which adultery is given as grounds for divorce, the co-respondent is the person with whom the respondent is alleged to have committed adultery.

What is the prayer?
The formal language of the petition is illustrated by a section on the last page. The petitioner 'prays' (i.e. asks) that the marriage be dissolved. In addition to this formal request, the petitioner can append a long list of other requests, for example, that the respondent pay the cost of the divorce, and make financial provision for the petitioner. The list will probably be a considerable set of demands – not all of which the petitioner expects to get. The aim of this is to leave as many as possible of the petitioner's options open at this stage, and not limit them by failing to ask for enough. If you ask for something now, it can save time and awkwardness later – even though you may not expect all your demands to be met at this stage.

What can I do if I am served with a petition?
As the respondent, you will receive not only the petition but also an **acknowledgement-of-service** form. This must be completed and returned to the court within eight days. The form contains questions about your responses to the costs requests made by the petitioner.

You will be asked if you intend to defend the divorce. Most people do not because they are content for the divorce to go through, and defending a divorce is a very expensive business. However, you might object to some of the details given in support of the fact – for example, details of supposedly 'unreasonable' behaviour. You should discuss these objections with your solicitor, and, if possible, your spouse, to try to work out an acceptable compromise.

What is the 'Statement of Arrangements for Children'?

This is a statement that accompanies the petition and provides information on the children of the marriage. It sets out the following:

- where each child is going to live
- the type of accommodation each child is going to live in
- whom the child is going to live with
- the school or educational establishment the child attends
- what financial arrangements have been made for the child, and what arrangements have been planned for the future
- what arrangements have been made for the child's welfare, and what arrangements have been planned for the future.

What happens when the respondent acknowledges the service of the petition?

The court sends a copy of the acknowledgement to the petitioner, who can then proceed to the next stage, probably with the help of a solicitor. This is to apply for **directions for trial**. In order to do this, the petitioner completes a **directions-for-trial (special-procedure) form** and also completes an affidavit relevant to the grounds given in the petition. There are separate **forms of affidavit of evidence** for each of the five grounds and a form needs to be completed for each of the grounds stated in the petition – although there is normally only one. The petitioner will also confirm whether he or she will be pursuing a claim for costs.

When all the necessary documentation has been received and checked by the district judge, a date will be fixed by the court office for the pronouncement of the **decree nisi** by the judge in court.

What is a decree nisi?

'Nisi' is the Latin for 'unless'. A decree nisi is therefore an interim stage in a divorce. It is an order for divorce that will not be made absolute unless certain procedures are complied with. A decree nisi is made by the court and, although you will be informed of the date, you will not have to attend. As well as considering that there is adequate evidence of the breakdown of the marriage for the pronouncement of the decree nisi, the judge will consider the arrangements for the children. If these arrangements are seen as satisfactory, the judge will certify that you are entitled to a decree nisi.

What is the judge looking at when he or she looks at the arrangements for the children?

The 'Statement of Arrangements for the Children' will already have been completed by the petitioner. If you and your spouse can agree on what should happen to the children, then both of you will have signed this. However, even if you both agree about matters such as where the children should live and the details of the contact they should have with the absent parent, the judge will still have to consider whether these are the best arrangements possible, in the interests of the children. The Children Act of 1989 states that the welfare of the children should be the most important factor in deciding matters of residence and contact. If the judge is satisfied with these arrangements, a certificate (called a **Section 41 certificate**) will be issued. The date for the pronouncement of the decree nisi can then be fixed.

What happens if we can't agree on arrangements for our children?

If you cannot agree on what should happen with the children, then the respondent can file his or her own statement. You might disagree on where the children should live, for example, or how often the absent parent should have contact. One of you might ask for a **Section 8 order** (called after the relevant section of the Children Act) to be made on any of these aspects. Bear in mind that the judge will make such an order only if it is in the best interests of the child or children. Before doing so, the judge might ask that a welfare report be prepared. This will be prepared by a court welfare officer, who will interview both spouses, talk to the children, and make other enquiries, which will help in deciding the outcome (for example, getting information from schools and interviewing family members such as grandparents). You and your spouse will receive a copy of this report.

The welfare officer may include a recommendation as to what arrangements would be best for the children. The court does not have to accept this recommendation, but it will give it very serious consideration. Instead of asking for such a report to be prepared, the judge may instead ask you and your spouse to use the court's conciliation service to see if you can arrive at a compromise over the dispute. If, as a result of this mediation, the judge thinks an order is still appropriate, then one will be made. If he or she thinks it is now unnecessary, then a certificate will be issued to that effect. In either case, a date can now be fixed for the pronouncement of the decree nisi.

How do I get a decree absolute?

Once the decree nisi has been granted and arrangements for the children have been approved, then a period of six weeks must normally elapse before the petitioner can apply for a decree absolute. Unless such an application is made, the decree absolute will not be granted. If the petitioner does not apply, then a period of three months must elapse before the respondent can apply, in turn. Once a decree absolute is obtained, the marriage is dissolved and both parties are free to remarry. For most people, this moment is one of profound relief that the whole thing is over, and that normal life can now be resumed!

Once I have started divorce proceedings, can I stop them?

Yes, at any time, short of the making of the decree absolute. All you have to do is inform the court, or your solicitor if you are using one. Surprisingly, as many as 20 per cent of couples who start divorce proceedings don't complete them!

Do I have to pay to start divorce proceedings?

Unless you are on a low income, you will have to pay a small fee. The court or your solicitor will notify you of the amount.

How much will a divorce cost me?

This is impossible to say with any accuracy, as costs can vary so greatly, depending on the length of the process and on the calibre of the legal representation! However, it should be borne in mind that the divorce itself will probably be the cheapest item on the bill, compared with other aspects of the divorce procedure: property arrangements, loss of income due to changed circumstances, maintenance payments for the children and so on. If you are in dispute with your spouse over a lot of issues, you will be using up more of your solicitor's time – with resulting expense. An hourly rate of between £100 and £300 per hour for solicitors is not uncommon. However, you can ask to use more junior partners in a firm, in order to reduce costs, if this is a problem. And some solicitors are happy to be paid in instalments – but check first!

What is Legal Aid?

Legal Aid is a system of different schemes enabling those on low incomes to obtain the services of a solicitor. For divorce cases, the relevant ones are:

- **Legal Aid and Assistance** (the 'Green Form' scheme). This covers help from a solicitor such as advice, writing letters and negotiating up to a fixed amount of time – at present, three hours.
- **Assistance by Way of Representation.** This covers a solicitor's costs involved in the preparation of and representation in a case that is being heard in a magistrates' court or Family Proceedings Court.
- **Civil Legal Aid.** This covers all the work necessary for cases being heard in county courts and Family Proceedings Courts. It will include all the work necessary for the preparation of the case and also representation by a solicitor.
- **The Fixed Fee Interview.** Some solicitors operate this scheme, which offers a brief period of legal advice (say, half an hour) for a low, fixed fee. This scheme applies to everyone, regardless of whether you are entitled to any of the other schemes.

How do I know if I am entitled to Legal Aid?

A solicitor will help you fill in the application form and will be able to tell you if you are entitled to help, taking into account your income and savings. Or you can check this for yourself, in *A Practical Guide to Legal Aid* (see Suggested Reading).

Getting the right solicitor for you

If it's clear that divorce is the only option, then you need to think about getting the appropriate legal advice to suit your circumstances. If you and your partner are agreed that you want to separate, and simply need help working out the financial aspects of this, then a 'do-it-yourself' divorce is relatively easy. If you can sort out your affairs with the help of a mediator, then so much the better. Increasingly, more and more people are choosing to do this, in order to avoid both financial costs and the adversarial approach adopted by some lawyers on behalf of their clients, which can, in some instances, make things more acrimonious. If, however, there is little or no common ground between you and your partner, then you will almost certainly need a solicitor's help.

Before seeking it, ask yourself what kind of legal assistance you really want. Do you want someone to 'fight' for you, or are you in need of sound advice, in order to guide you through the pitfalls of separation and to prevent you giving up rights through ignorance of the law? Bear in mind that the more contentious the divorce, the higher the legal costs are likely to be. And, while a solicitor's services can be invaluable in working out an equitable settlement between you and your partner, they can also add to the tension already existing between a divorcing couple, as the partners score points off each other, using their solicitors as go-betweens – a very nasty and extremely expensive game of ping-pong!

When my friend Kathryn's marriage broke down, she and her husband, Peter, decided initially to negotiate a settlement themselves, without resorting to solicitors. 'I see now that I was incredibly naïve,' she says. 'But at the time neither of us was involved with anyone else, and things were fairly amicable between us.' Everything was fine until Kathryn started living with Alex, a colleague at the college of further education where she is a lecturer. 'As soon as Pete found out about me and Alex, all hell broke loose,' she recalls. 'Overnight, the payments Pete had been making towards our two children's maintenance stopped. When I rang him about it, he told me I didn't "need" his money any more, as I now had Alex to keep me! The joke is that Alex earns less than I do – but, in any case, Pete had an obligation towards George and Toby, our sons, until at least they finished full-time education. I was determined not to let Pete get out of his responsibility that easily!'

Kathryn enlisted the aid of the Child Support Agency, which brought a successful prosecution against her former husband. He was ordered to pay costs, and a maintenance agreement was reached, which worked out as slightly more than the amount Pete had originally been paying for the children's upkeep. 'Of course he never paid it,' Kathryn says ruefully. 'Almost immediately after we'd agreed the maintenance, Pete left his job at the newspaper where he'd been working as a journalist, and decided to go freelance. He was suddenly earning far less – which meant he couldn't keep up the payments at the agreed level. Then he met somebody else and she got pregnant. His argument was he now had two families to support on half an income. I lost count of the number of solicitor's letters that flew back and forth between the two sides. It all got very expensive – and of course it didn't improve relations between me and Pete. He was trying to punish me for getting involved with someone else, and I was furious with him for trying to duck out of his financial responsibilities towards me and the kids. It was a nightmare.'

Kathryn now feels that it would have been better to have come to a formal arrangement regarding the children's welfare through a solicitor, at a time when she and Peter were still on relatively good terms. 'We chose not to do so because of the expense,' she admits. 'It seemed like a good idea to just leave things on a "goodwill" basis, because we both thought that's how it would continue. But, when feelings are involved, people don't always make very fair or rational decisions. The irony is that both Pete and I have ended up much worse off – both financially and emotionally – than we would have done if we'd sorted it all out sooner.'

Adele, another friend, was able to consult a solicitor friend on an informal basis when she and her partner, Geoff, were thinking of splitting up. 'Both of us were reluctant to get into the whole legal adversarial thing,' she recalls. 'So it was incredibly lucky that I had Sally – my solicitor friend – to talk to. She advised me to get a solicitor we'd both agreed on to draw up a draft agreement, which Geoff and I could then look at, and decide if either of us wanted any modifications. That way, we would both have the advantage of having a legal expert sort out our finances and property matters, without having to retain two lawyers. It actually worked really well, because neither of us was out to hurt the other one financially. We just wanted a fair division of our joint assets. And I felt a lot happier, not because I didn't trust Geoff, but because I've never been very good with filling in forms and the like, and would have hated to have to do the whole legal bit myself. This was a good compromise.'

A solicitor should be able to discuss your position dispassionately and advise you on the best course of action to take. When faced with the breakdown of your marriage, you are likely to be in an emotional state; a good solicitor will be aware of this, and will try to calm the situation down wherever possible, offering rational advice that will benefit you and your children, and cautioning you against having unrealistic expectations. A solicitor will also try to impress upon you the importance of cooperation and help you to negotiate an agreement with your partner about finances. He or she may be able to:

- **put an agreement into wording** that will be clear to both parties and acceptable to the court
- **arrange maintenance** and the division of property in a more tax-efficient way
- **draw up a 'clean-break'** settlement where appropriate (e.g. when there are no children)
- **draw attention** to things you might not have realised (e.g. that a wife may lose pension rights under her husband's pension scheme).

Finding a solicitor

Citizens' Advice Bureaux, public libraries and court offices throughout the UK all have lists of practising solicitors in a given area, published in the Law Society's Regional Directories. These will also give details of lawyers willing to do legal aid work. (The CAB will be able to tell you if you are eligible for Legal Aid.) When you telephone or write to a firm of solicitors, remember to ask them if they have someone who specialises in matrimonial cases. For preference, he or she should be a member of the Solicitors Family Law Association (SFLA). This is an organisation of around 5,000 lawyers who have a code of practice designed to encourage people to reach acceptable agreements for the future in as positive and conciliatory (rather than aggressive and litigious) a way as possible. You may even find SFLA solicitors listed in the Yellow Pages. When visiting your solicitor for the first time, it may be helpful to draw up a checklist of essential information you will need to produce, to save time (and money) at your appointment:

- **your marriage certificate**
- **a summary of your financial position** (including details of your and your spouse's income from work or welfare benefits; details of your home and its approximate value; any other capital assets and any debts and liabilities)
- **the names and ages of your children**, as well as details of any children of previous marriages
- **your name, address, date of birth, occupation**, and any other relevant data (such as whether you have been married before, plus the date and circumstances of the earlier divorce)
- **any correspondence** you may have received from your partner's solicitor.

It is also a good idea to open your own file of relevant documents at home, so that you can always lay your hands on any essential bit of information. This can also help to keep track of solicitors' costs – remember that you can ask for an interim assessment of how much your case is costing if this is not supplied automatically. A good solicitor should also send you a 'client care' letter, outlining the firm's code of practice. This is meant to 'ensure that the client who is unfamiliar with the law and lawyers receives the information he or she needs to make what is happening more comprehensible and thus to reduce areas of potential conflict and complaint'. Bear in mind that your solicitor is there to help you. If you are not satisfied with the service you are receiving, or if you wish to change solicitors, you can apply to the Office for the Supervision of Solicitors (OSS) for their leaflet *What to do if you are dissatisfied with your solicitor*. Remember, a good solicitor should help you achieve the kind of divorce you want.

What should I expect from my solicitor?

Good solicitors should always act in your best interests. They should explain to you your rights, and the rights of the other side, and should advise you against pursuing an unwise claim or argument. You should always be satisfied that your solicitor is bringing his or her full professional expertise to bear on your case, and is defending your rights as vigorously as possible.

The Solicitors Family Law Association

This association of around 5,000 solicitors experienced in matrimonial law, favours a conciliatory approach in divorce cases, which is governed by a **Code of Practice**. This states:

- that the interests of children should always be the first concern
- that a family dispute should be approached as a search for fair solutions, rather than a contest to produce a winner and a loser
- that child-related issues should be kept separate from financial issues

- that the solicitor should avoid heightening personal emotions
- that the solicitor should encourage full, frank and clear disclosure of information
- that the solicitor should ensure that the client is aware of services such as mediation
- that before taking any step, such as filing a petition, the solicitor should consider informing the other party – especially if such a step might be misunderstood or construed as hostile.

This commitment to reducing the level of hostility does not mean that the SFLA solicitor cannot take 'immediate and decisive action' when required. The association stresses, 'Adherence to the Code is not a sign of weakness, nor does it expose the client to disadvantage.' In other words, conciliation is not a sign that you are 'giving in' to the other side's demands, but that, by trying to deal fairly and unemotionally with your former partner, through his/her legal representative, you are doing your utmost to take the heat out of the situation, and thus bring about a just settlement.

Domestic violence

Domestic violence occurs more frequently than any of us would care to admit. According to a recent survey, one in four of all reported crimes falls into this category, although the actual levels of this kind of crime – and it *is* a crime – are much harder to determine, because so many cases go unreported. Such incidents – which can range from slapping and punching to full-scale physical assaults that can leave the victim seriously injured or dead – often occur behind closed doors, with no witnesses present, and can go on for years, with one partner terrified into silence by the other's persistent abuse.

If this is your situation, you need to act quickly to protect yourself

– and your children if they are affected (and there is no way that they will *not* be affected; staying with a violent partner 'for the sake of the children' is never an acceptable option). Your first step should be to contact the police, who will, in extreme circumstances, remove the violent partner from the house. If violence has been merely threatened, not acted out, the police may be able to calm the situation down by talking separately to each partner, and trying to resolve the situation. If an assault has actually occurred, the police will consider whether criminal charges should be brought.

If you have reason to fear that contacting the police will result in further violence towards you or your children, you may find it preferable to remove yourself and your children from the house to a place of safety, such as a women's refuge (since the majority of cases of domestic violence – although by no means all – are inflicted by men upon women, I am assuming here that the victim is female). Although in principle, if you are instigating divorce proceedings, it is preferable to remain in the matrimonial home until an agreement has been reached, *in cases where violence is an issue, you should always put personal safety above legal or financial considerations.* But apply for legal advice as soon as possible, in order to safeguard your rights in the situation. Your local Citizens' Advice Bureau will be able to advise you on whether you are eligible for Legal Aid. If you have to apply for an injunction to prevent a violent partner molesting you, you may be eligible for Legal Aid to help with the cost of this.

There are two types of court order that can be obtained to prevent a violent spouse approaching you or your children – both of which are referred to as an 'injunction' (this just means an order by the court telling someone what he or she must or must not do, the penalty for disobeying which can be imprisonment). The two types are:

- **a nonmolestation injunction or personal protection order**
- **an ouster order or exclusion order**

A nonmolestation injunction orders the spouse not to assault, molest or pester you in any way. This includes unwanted telephone calls and other forms of harassment. An ouster injunction can order a spouse to leave the home and not come within a specified distance of it. Both are designed for the protection of you and your children.

In cases of actual physical injury to the applicant or a child, the court can attach a power of arrest to the order. This means that, once the offending spouse has been served with the order, he can be immediately arrested if it is breached (again, I am assuming here that the perpetrator of the violence is male). A power of arrest usually lasts for a fixed period of three months. It is in practice the most effective preventive action that can be taken against further violent attacks. However, it is important to bear in mind the consequences of seeking and obtaining an 'ouster' injunction, as regards your future relationship with your partner. If you are commencing divorce proceedings in this way, then it will become correspondingly harder to reach an amicable or negotiated settlement. In cases of extreme violence, you will, of course, have no choice but to proceed in this way.

If you have been injured in a recent assault by your spouse and wish to have this entered as evidence in court proceedings, you should go immediately to your doctor or local casualty department, where you will be examined by a qualified medical practitioner and your injuries noted on your medical records. A solicitor may even ask your doctor to prepare a report on your injuries, for which a small fee may be charged.

One common effect of the kind of relentless physical and mental cruelty to which some people – generally women – are subjected within long-term relationships is that the victim herself may feel she is in some way to 'blame' for the abuse. Studies have shown that this self-punishing attitude can arise when an individual's self-esteem has been undermined to the extent that she believes that she deserves nothing better.

Linda, who left her violent marriage eight years ago, after her husband's repeated abuse put her in hospital on several occasions, remembers how humiliated she felt by his treatment. 'That was almost as bad as the actual hitting – the way he'd go on and on about how worthless and fat and stupid I was. It got so that I'd believe it myself. My sister used to say, "You must be mad to stay with him." And I did feel she must be right: I *was* mad. Mad and stupid.'

The abuse began when Trevor, Linda's husband, lost his job, and they were forced to sell the house they'd saved up for years to buy. 'Trev started drinking heavily. He got very depressed. One day, I was cooking his tea and I said something he didn't like and he just took the pan of eggs and bacon and threw it at the wall. Later, he started throwing things at me – knives, forks, stuff like that. I was five months pregnant when he started hitting me.'

Linda now feels that the pregnancy – which was unplanned – was the event that tipped the scales as far as her relationship with Trevor was concerned. 'He'd always been moody, but never violent. Having Natalie changed all that. He never touched her, but if the least thing upset him, he started on me. It was slapping at first; later it got to punching and kicking. I used to have to wear long sleeves all the time to hide the bruises.'

Eventually, after one assault left her with a broken jaw, Linda took Natalie and went to stay with her mother, telling Trevor she wanted a divorce. 'He turned up the next day with flowers and a present for Natalie, saying he was sorry and it wouldn't happen again. The thing is, I really think he meant it, at one level. Trevor can be very charming when he wants to be. So I went back to him. But a few months later he lost his temper during a row about money, and hit me again. I decided I wanted out.'

Afraid that Trevor's violence towards her might be exacerbated during the divorce proceedings, Linda obtained a court order against him, preventing him from visiting her or their daughter for three months. 'The day the injunction ran out, I had a phone call from Trevor, saying he'd enrolled with Alcoholics Anonymous, and had given up drinking. He'd also had some counselling to combat his violent tendencies. He wanted me to take him back – but I didn't believe he'd changed as much as he said, underneath. Those three months helped me see that I was better off without him.'

If, like Linda, you are suffering from persistent mental or physical abuse by a spouse, your self-esteem will be low, and your confidence nil. You may be too frightened or ashamed to tell anyone else what is going on. You may even feel your partner has a 'right' to treat you in this way, simply because he is your partner. This is nonsense. No one has the right to treat another person badly. In certain cases, two people who are sufficiently committed to a relationship in which one or both of the partners have behaved violently can undergo therapy in order that this cycle of behaviour can be broken, and the relationship survive. This has to be done in a controlled way, preferably under supervision by a qualified person, such as a psychiatrist.

Most abusers claim that they 'won't do it again' – but this isn't something you can afford to leave to chance. If you are in a violent relationship – or know of someone else who is – the first course of action is to get yourself (or your acquaintance) out of harm's way as soon as possible. The second is to consult a solicitor as to your best course of action, to protect you and your children against the abuser. Remember, you have a right to a decent life, free from fear and the threat of physical harm. It may seem, at present, virtually impossible to achieve this – but, believe me, you can. A better life may be just a phone call away.

4

How Do We Tell the Children?

Divorce is a painful process, and one of the most difficult things about it is breaking the news to a child or children that you and your partner have decided to separate. Even when the strains in a marriage have become all too apparent to the parents themselves, children often find it hard to believe that anything is wrong – ironically, because the parents may have made efforts not to row in front of them. For very young children, unsettled by any disruption of their familiar routine, it may be hard to understand that Daddy (or Mummy) isn't going to be there as much as he or she used to be; older children may retreat into silence, or display violent mood swings – alternating between exaggeratedly affectionate, 'clingy' behaviour and hostility. Some may even blame themselves for the break-up.

A child's initial reaction may be one of sheer disbelief, or even flat denial. They may act as if nothing had happened – a reaction that can be disconcerting to parents who have made efforts to break the news gently. 'When Ian and I split up, we were determined to do it in as civilised a way as possible,' recalls Sarah, a GP. 'We told the children we wanted to talk to them, and then we all sat down together around the kitchen table. I remember that Matthew, who was nine at the time, was playing with one of his Lego cars – running it up and down the table while Ian and I were talking. Emily, our daughter, who was

For children to deny that something unpleasant has happened
is a common defence strategy.

twelve at the time, was quite upset when she realised that Ian was
going to be moving out, but Matthew didn't react at all. He just
kept on playing with his car, and, when we ran out of things to
say, he said "Can I go now?" and went to his room.'

Denying that something unpleasant has happened is a common
defensive strategy, which children and adults alike can adopt
when events are too much for them to cope with. Faced with the
uncompromising fact of their parents' divorce, some children
may become withdrawn and quiet, refusing to discuss what has
happened, and resisting any attempt on the part of the adults to
get them to talk about their feelings. Others may demonstrate
their hurt and anger in more direct ways, becoming difficult to
deal with, if not actually aggressive.

'Caitlin went almost overnight from being the easiest child –
no trouble at home or at school – to behaving like an absolute
brat,' says Jane, a speech therapist. 'There was a lot of acrimony

when Rob and I broke up, and I think she must have soaked it up, poor kid. She started truanting from school, and spending a lot of time at friends' houses, without telling me where she was going. Her schoolwork suffered, and she started getting a reputation as a bit of a troublemaker. When I confronted her about her behaviour, she'd just scream at me, storm off to her room and slam her door. It was hell for a while. The worst of it was, I was still so angry at Rob that I couldn't see how much Caitlin was suffering because of it. The two people she'd loved and trusted most in the world had let her down, and she wanted everyone to know how angry she was.'

Both Caitlin and her mother have since had family therapy, and found it helped to break through the wall of silence that had grown up between them since Jane and Rob divorced. 'Suddenly, Caitlin was talking to me again, and it was absolutely wonderful. I realised how uncertain she must have been that she was still loved, and that her confrontational behaviour was just her way of trying to provoke a reaction.' Caitlin, now fourteen, is settled at a new school, and Jane and Rob have made efforts to reconcile their differences over the areas that concern their daughter's future. 'Rob and I will never be friends, but at least we don't have to act like enemies in front of our child,' says Jane. 'Our problems with each other are nothing to do with Caitlin, and she shouldn't have been made to feel she was in any way responsible.'

The crucial thing to remember when you are going through the early stages of a separation is that, even though you and your partner may no longer want to be together, your status as parents doesn't alter. In fact, one might go as far as to say that, for divorced parents, the responsibilities of parenthood have to be taken even more seriously than they do when both parents are living in the family home. For any couple in the throes of separation, spending time with their children suddenly becomes all-important. When everything seems in turmoil, maintaining the ordinary rituals of bathtimes and bedtimes and helping with homework can provide a reassuring sense of continuity for adults and children alike.

So just how *do* you go about telling your children that you and your partner are going to live apart? And how do you minimise the damage caused by such a revelation? Well, the first thing to say is that, while there is no 'right' or 'wrong' way of approaching this, it is probably best to be in as calm a frame of mind as possible. Don't, in other words, do it when you have just been having a bitter row with your partner, and tempers are high. Remember, this isn't about you and your partner: it is about your children's peace of mind. You owe it to them to behave like rational people. Secondly, try to ensure that both you and your partner are present when you talk to your children. Present, as far as possible, a united front. Nothing is more confusing and upsetting to a child than conflicting information. Give them *one* set of reasons why you have decided to separate, not two different versions.

Avoid, above all, allowing any kind of personal abuse between the two of you to take place in front of your children. Even if one of you feels betrayed and angry with the other, there is no need to drag this up in talking to your children. While they may be able to accept that Mummy and Daddy no longer want to be together, it may come as an altogether more unpleasant shock to learn that Mummy and Daddy can't stand the sight of each other. How much you tell your children about what is actually going on between the two of you depends entirely on the age they are. Very young children will probably find it hard to grasp more than the basic fact that Daddy or Mummy isn't going to be living with them any more; older children will be able to cope with slightly more information; while teenagers (for whom divorce will already be a familiar topic) may need to discuss the whys and wherefores in considerable detail.

Whatever age your children are, the most important thing to keep in mind is that they need to be reassured that you both still love them. Make sure they know that – no matter what else has changed about the family set-up – your love and concern for them will never change. Don't make them 'choose' between one of you and the other. They're entitled to two parents, just like everyone else. Tell them that, just because you've decided to live apart, it doesn't mean they won't have access to both of you, as before. Try to address their fears – just because children don't voice their concerns, doesn't mean they don't have them. These may range from quite serious worries that they won't be 'allowed' to visit their grandparents any more to more minor things. The point is, it's up to you and your partner to set their minds at rest.

Whatever age your children are, it is probably better to avoid telling them the news of your impending break-up just before bedtime, when they will be left alone with the information all night, with predictably upsetting consequences. Instead, choose a time when there is plenty of opportunity to talk, so that every member of the family can air their concerns and fears about the future. Remember, they will almost certainly want to know why their parents are separating, and won't be content with the simple explanation that 'it's something your father [or mother] and I think will be for the best'.

You should tell your children that the decision has not been taken lightly, and that you have thought about it long and hard. You could say that you have both tried very hard to make things better between you, but that this has not worked out. Above all, you should emphasise that there are different kinds of love, and that, just because you and your partner no longer love each other in the same way, it does not mean that you have stopped loving them. This is the single most important thing you need to say to your children. You must reassure them that their needs are what come first for both of you, and that, as far as possible, you will continue to act together as their parents. Children are literal-minded beings, and – reasonably enough, when dealing with something they can't hope to understand – often tend to focus on minor or apparently trivial worries.

One friend's daughter, aged eleven at the time of her parents' separation, remained quiet all the time they were explaining the situation to her, and then burst out, 'I suppose this means you won't be coming to hear me play.' This referred to the clarinet solo she was due to perform in a school concert. Another friend's child wept inconsolably when it dawned on her that Daddy might not be there to pick her up from the class trip she was going on with her friends. Such worries, which may seem insignificant to you compared with the far more major trauma you and your partner are experiencing, are not insignificant to your child. He or she will want reassurance that, in little things as well as great, life will go on much as it has before, and that, just because you and Daddy (or Mummy) are about to make changes in your arrangements, this does not mean that everything else has to change.

Do's and don'ts of telling your children about divorce

- **Do** explain things in as lucid and calm a way as possible.
- **Do** give them one set of reasons for the break-up – not several conflicting ones.
- **Do** tell them how much you love them.
- **Do** give them a chance to voice their concerns.
- **Do** tell them as soon as you can – putting off the awful moment will only make it harder for all of you.

- **Don't** indulge in name-calling or recrimination in front of them.
- **Don't** make them choose between one parent and the other.
- **Don't** expect them to take in the news straight away.
- **Don't** tell them at bedtime – give them time to adjust beforehand.

- **Don't** say, 'You know when you fall out with friends sometimes, and then you're not friends any more – well, it's like that with me and Daddy [or Mummy]...' It *isn't* like that. Children generally make up with their friends after a quarrel. You and your partner are not going to – at least, not in any way that makes sense to a child.

'When Martin and I first discussed our separation with the children, he'd already moved out,' recalls Emma, a lecturer in ceramics at an art college. 'They knew something was up, because he'd been spending so much time away from the house, but even so it was a shock to them. Rosie, our elder daughter, who was ten, burst into tears when I said that Dad wasn't going to be living with us any more. Our younger one, Grace, kept saying, "What did you *do*, Mummy?" – which was actually quite funny, as Martin had been the one to leave. Martin hadn't wanted to say anything about the fact that he was living with somebody else, because he thought it might prejudice the girls against him – but then Rosie came right out with it and said, "Dad, have you got a girlfriend?"'

Emma and Martin had agreed to give their daughters a simplified version of the reasons for their break-up, mainly because neither was entirely sure that the separation was going to be permanent. 'We told the girls we needed some time apart, to decide if we wanted to go on being together,' says Emma. 'We said that Dad would still be coming to the house every day, and that he'd go on picking them up from school. We went so far in that direction – trying to reassure them that nothing was really going to change – that they found it quite hard to understand why we were separating at all. I remember Rosie saying something like, "If you still love each other, and you love us, and we're going to see Dad every day – then why can't things just stay the way they were?" Kids are so logical.'

One of the things that worried eight-year-old Grace was that she might be ostracised by her friends at school if they found out that her parents were no longer together. 'She kept saying, "I don't want to be the one with no Daddy,"' recalls Emma. 'It was heartbreaking.' Even though divorce is far more widespread, and more children are being brought up in single-parent households than ever before, the idea that there is something shameful and 'different' about coming from a broken home still persists – an idea often reinforced by the stereotypical nuclear families of children's television and advertising. 'We pointed out that Grace's best friend, Zoe, lives with her mum and sees her dad only at weekends. That cheered her up a bit,' says Emma. 'But it was still a long time before she said anything about Martin not living with us any more to any of her friends.'

Teresa's children were teenagers when she and Richard decided to part. 'Claire had just done her A-levels, and I remember thinking it was a bit much to spring it on her, after having to go through all that – but she was absolutely fine about it. Being the eldest, she'd picked up quite a bit of what was going on between me and Richard, and I don't think it came as much of a surprise to her. She's always had a good relationship with her father, and, when I made it clear that he and I would still be friends, I think it was a great relief to her. Neither Richard nor I would have wanted a situation which made things uncomfortable for the children.'

Luke, the couple's fifteen-year-old, was initially the one who reacted badly. 'He was very angry with Richard, and wouldn't speak to him for several days. Even after they were speaking again, the relationship remained frosty for quite a while. I think Luke and his father are actually fairly alike in temperament, and that makes it difficult for them to see the other's point of view. Nicholas, our thirteen-year-old, was much more laid back about the whole thing.'

Much has been written in recent years about the traumatic effects of divorce upon children. According to this analysis, broken marriages are directly responsible for all kinds of social ills affecting young people – from vandalism to poor attainment levels at school. While there is obviously some truth in all this, it may be more accurate to say that divorce itself is a *consequence* of wider social breakdown, not a cause. And certainly, no one with any sense would want to return to the bad old days when people stayed together 'because of the children', or make it more difficult for, say, a woman trapped in a violent marriage to escape it. And, while most studies that have been done over the past twenty years or so agree that divorce can have a detrimental effect on a child's self-esteem and academic attainment in the immediate aftermath of the break-up, there is also a growing understanding that it is not the *event* of divorce that is harmful so much as what precedes it, and how it is handled afterwards. If divorce is handled well, children can deal with it well.

Few would question that the ideal arrangement in which to bring up children is still the two-parent family. No one, given the choice, wants to make life less than ideal for their children. That is why it is usually only when every alternative has been considered that most parents decide to divorce. When things have broken down so much between you and your partner that you can no longer sustain a loving and supportive environment for your children, then divorce becomes the lesser of two evils. For children who have lived in the shadow of an unhappy relationship, their parents' decision to separate can come as an enormous relief.

For Ella, now in her mid-twenties, whose parents divorced when she was thirteen, it meant the end of what had come to seem an intolerable situation: 'Basically, my dad was like Jekyll and Hyde – really charming and lovely when he wasn't drinking, and an absolute pig when he was drunk. He made Mum's life a misery a lot of the time. When my brother and I were smaller, it wasn't so bad – or maybe we just didn't notice as much. But when we got to be a bit older it was really horrible. He'd come home from lunching with clients already half drunk; then he'd carry on drinking throughout the evening. I don't think he ever physically abused my mother, but he was just very nasty to her. Sneering and sarcastic – always telling her what a useless person she was. He used to take it out on my brother, too. It made a terrible atmosphere in the house.'

Ella has no doubt that the divorce was a good thing – especially for her mother. 'I think she'd been so worn down by the strain of living with my father's moods all those years that, when they eventually split up, it was like a new life for her. Being told she was incompetent and hopeless had really undermined her confidence. When my father left, she could be her own person again. She started making new friends, which she'd never had when my father was around, and even learned to drive – it was incredible!'

Ironically enough, the change in Ella's mother so impressed her father that he suggested at one stage that they should get back together for a trial period. 'Mum told me afterwards that she'd considered it very seriously, partly because of us – my brother and me – and partly because she remembered how good their marriage had been in the early days. My father even promised to quit drinking if she'd have him back. But in the end, I think she no longer trusted him enough.'

Ella's father did eventually take steps to deal with his alcoholism, and her mother has since remarried. 'It wasn't exactly a "happy ending", but it's worked out better than either of them could have expected. In their case, divorce was a real lifesaver.'

Natasha, now nineteen, is matter-of-fact about being the child of divorced parents. 'It's almost as if people like me are the "normal" ones, these days,' she says. 'When I was at school, just about all my friends were from single-parent families, with parents who were either divorced or who'd never been married.

So there was never any embarrassment about it that I can recall.'
Natasha was eight when her parents separated, so her memories
of the time leading up to the divorce are fairly hazy. 'I don't
remember my parents having serious fights, or anything like that.
They always seemed quite friendly when my sister and I were
around. But I know now that they'd been going to relationship
counselling for several months before my dad moved out. The
most Mum's ever said was that she and my dad had "grown
apart" as people, and that they both felt they needed to develop
their lives in different directions.'

Because her parents remained on amicable terms both during
the divorce and after it, Natasha doesn't feel that she has been
'torn apart' by the separation. 'My sister and I were never forced
to "choose" between our parents. Mum was always keen for us to
spend time with Dad at weekends and holidays – although in
practice we saw less of him because he was away on business
such a lot. But my parents were never bitter or sarcastic about
each other, the way some people's parents are when the marriage
ends.' Natasha does feel that having divorced parents has affected
her own views on marriage, however. 'I suppose I'm more wary
than many people my age are, because of the divorce. I don't
really see myself settling down with anyone until I'm at least
thirty. I want to do a lot more with my life than that! But then I
think the whole idea of marriage as a goal for women has
changed since our parents' day.'

For young women like Ella and Natasha, who have coped
well with their parents' divorce, what must once have seemed
a terrible, earth-shattering event has now – quite rightly –
receded into the past. Both have been able to get on with their
lives, without feeling they have suffered too much damage.
Both are capable, as they enter adult life, of feeling some
sympathy with their parents, and of understanding the reasons
why it was necessary for them to part. Obviously, not all young
adults emerge unscathed from the experience of divorce; but,

without overstating the case, it should be borne in mind that children are often more resilient than their parents imagine. They, too, are capable of dealing with divorce in the best way – by moving on.

5
Telling Family and Friends

After telling the children, breaking the news that you and your partner have decided to separate to your respective families is one of the most traumatic things you will have to face during the early stages of a divorce. This may be because it is the first step on the road to 'going public' – a point of no return, after which you, as a couple, will cease to exist as such in the eyes of the rest of the world. Many couples going through a difficult period in their married lives will have struggled to keep their problems a secret, not only from their children, but also from parents and other family members; so it may come as much more of a shock when, having delayed the moment of truth as long as possible, you decide to 'come clean' with your nearest and dearest.

For the older generation, especially, there may be a considerable stigma attached to the idea of divorce. Quite apart from any religious scruples that may be an issue, there is the idea – shared by many – that divorce is a form of 'failure', and therefore something to be ashamed of. Most parents, confronted with the news that their son's or daughter's marriage has broken down, will offer nothing but sympathy and understanding. But be prepared for dismay, shock, incomprehension – even anger. And, again, stay as calm as you can – even in the face of an unsympathetic reaction.

'When I rang my mother to say that Rob had left, I was

expecting her to say how sorry she was that my marriage was over,' says Jane. 'But all she said was, "You had to put me through this, didn't you?" I was absolutely flabbergasted. According to her, I was getting divorced just to spite her!' Jane believes that, subconsciously, her mother may have been venting her own feelings of frustration over her own unsatisfactory marriage. 'She and my father were never really happy together. I think, at one level, she actually envied me, because I'd had the courage to do what she'd never dared to do – get out of a bad relationship.'

For parents who have themselves been through a divorce, learning that their child, too, is about to undergo the trauma of separation can come as all the more of a shock. 'My mother started crying and saying, "I've let you down, I've let you down,"' recalls Sarah, whose parents were also divorced when she was in her teens. 'It took me quite a long time to persuade her that it wasn't her "fault" that Ian and I had decided to part, and that she hadn't set me a "bad example" by divorcing Dad. Funnily enough, Ian's parents – who've been happily married for yonks – were much more philosophical about it. Ian's mother came out with all these wonderful homilies like "It's no use crying over spilt milk" and "Worse things happen at sea." She was so calm and stoical about it, that it made *me* want to cry.'

Because Sarah's mother and stepfather live quite a distance away from them, Sarah broke the news to her mother on the telephone – a mistake, she now feels. 'It's so difficult to gauge another person's reactions on the phone. And you can't give them a hug when they're upset. We took the time to go and visit Ian's parents, who live fairly close by. I think they realised something was up, because we weren't "due" for a visit – and we'd left the children with friends for the day,' says Sarah. 'My father-in-law's first words when we arrived were, "You know your mother and I don't want to pry, but if there's anything we can do . . . " I think he thought Ian had got the sack, or something.'

Breaking the news face to face was hard, but at least, Sarah feels, it got everything that needed to be said out in the open. 'My mother-in-law kept asking us if we were "sure" we'd made the right decision, and if we'd thought about the consequences for the children. When she realised that we'd thought everything through pretty carefully, she just said, "Well, you must do what you have to do." '

For many divorcing couples, of course, the idea of making a joint announcement of the proposed separation to parents and friends isn't something either would feel comfortable with. Nor would it be practical in a lot of cases – for instance where one partner has already left the marital home. What is most likely to happen in these circumstances is for each partner to 'tell' his or her respective parents and close friends. Gemma remembers phoning her parents shortly after Paul left to live with his girlfriend, Sara. 'It was my father who answered the phone. As soon as I heard his voice, I burst into tears and couldn't speak. He said, "Do you want to talk about it, or shall I ring you back when you've had a chance to calm down?" I was a complete basket case. The thing is, I'd had to be so calm and collected about what was happening because of the children. Telling my own parents was like going back to being a child myself. I felt I didn't have to pretend any more. I could just give in to my feelings.'

Louise, whose relationship with her mother is 'more like that of sisters than mother and daughter', was able to be very direct when it came to telling her the bad news about her marriage. 'I usually ring her once a week, and we just chat about this and that – work, and other members of the family and so on. On this occasion, we'd been talking about not very much and Liz, my mother, suddenly said, "How's John?" I said, "It's funny you should mention John, because he and I have decided to spend some time apart for a while." Liz wasn't fazed in the least. She just said, "Fine. That sounds like a good idea to me." And then we carried on chatting about other things.'

Liz, herself a divorcee, admits that she was more upset at the news than she let on at first. 'Of course I was a bit shaken. Who wouldn't be, hearing that a child was having a difficult time? But I remembered when I was going through my own divorce how much I hated people getting emotional about it – it seemed an intrusion, somehow. Louise is like me in that respect. She can't stand fuss. I knew she'd talk to me about it in her own time.'

For any concerned parent, hearing the news that their son or daughter is unhappily married is bound to be upsetting – even if, as was the case with Liz, it does not come entirely as a shock. 'Louise had confided in me that John wasn't so keen on having children,' she says. 'So I knew there were tensions in the marriage. But of course I'd hoped they might be able to work them out. When she told me they'd decided to separate, I knew things must have got pretty bad between them. Louise isn't a quitter. She'd have done anything to keep the marriage going. But having a child had become a real issue for her – and, perhaps selfishly, for me: I'd love a grandchild!'

If parental reactions to news of divorce can vary from outraged disapproval to sympathetic concern, the reactions of friends when you tell them you've decided to 'make a break' can be equally unpredictable. Lifelong friends can suddenly become cool and distant, while people you hardly know suddenly start treating you like their closest mate. There's no doubt that news of a divorce can polarise people, causing rifts between groups of friends, as some take sides with one half of a couple, some with the other. Sometimes this is because one partner may be perceived as having behaved badly to the other, and – rather than get into the minefield of who did what to whom – those who are friends of *both* parties prefer to sever the link altogether. Or it may be that they are just too embarrassed to get in touch, or feel *you* might be embarrassed to hear from them. Many couples – particularly those who may themselves have been going through a difficult time in their relationship – are unsettled by the idea of divorce, and may even fear it could be 'contagious'!

News of a divorce can polarise people, causing rifts between groups of friends, as some take sides with one half of a couple, some with the other.

'When Mark and I split up, I lost a whole group of friends,' recalls Nicola, who works for a firm of architects in Central London. 'We'd been married eight years, and – as young couples do – had built up quite a wide circle of friends, mainly other couples. Quite a number of these were work friends (Mark's job is in television), but, after we moved from our rather poky flat in Dalston to a house in London Fields, we started to do a lot more entertaining. I don't suppose there were many weekends that went by when we didn't have people round, for dinner parties or just to chat over a bottle of wine. Funnily enough, when Mark and I separated, it was these occasions I missed almost as much as our life together.'

Some of the friends Nicola no longer sees were colleagues of Mark's, who'd seen the connection with the couple as being through him, not her. Others, more surprisingly, were people she'd thought of as 'her' friends. 'One friend rang to say she'd like to invite me to her birthday party that weekend, but thought I'd probably prefer not to be there because she'd invited Mark. The hurtful thing was, she and I were at college together, and so I'd assumed she would want to go on being friends with me. But Mark and her husband work together, so she'd chosen not to offend *him*. Needless to say, I crossed *her* off my Christmas card list!'

Jen, a divorcee in her early thirties, feels that friends who have known you as one half of a couple often find it hard to relate to you as an individual. 'When I was married to Matt, we went everywhere together; all our friends were other couples, in similar circumstances to our own – two incomes, no kids. When we broke up, it was like, "Hello? Where did all my friends go?" Very few of the people we knew as a couple are still my friends now.' Jen thinks that this is because she and Matt went through their divorce at a time when several of the other couples in their group were deciding to have babies. 'I suppose, to be fair, they must have thought I'd be upset by all the broody, couply stuff that was going on – and so they just didn't invite me. I'd find out afterwards that someone had had a party, or that there'd been a group weekend away in France, and that I was the only one not to have been asked along. Strangely enough, it didn't seem to affect the way these particular friends treated Matt.'

Jen isn't alone in feeling that it is the female member of the partnership who often gets the cold shoulder from friends who had been common to both parties. 'It upset me at first,' she recalls, 'because I thought it meant there must be something wrong with *me*. Now I think it shows how threatened some of these people were by the idea of a single, independent woman disrupting their cosy little circle.' Several years on, Jen has made new friendships, with people who aren't fazed by her singleton status. 'The friends I've got now – some single, some couples – really see me as *me*, not as some sort of appendage to Matt. I still occasionally bump into the others, because we all live in the same area – and, when I do, I make sure to tell them what a brilliant time I'm having being single!'

6

'At Least You Haven't Got Kids...'

For couples who don't have children, breaking up has its own particular problems – the worst of which is probably dealing with other people's insensitive reactions to the news. When a couple with children separate, people display a natural concern for the innocent victims of the divorce; no one, it is reasonably supposed, would want to put their children through such a traumatic experience. Be that as it may, it doesn't necessarily follow that a childless couple who are undergoing divorce feel that they are 'better off' or 'lucky' not to have children. Some couples may indeed have split up over this very issue; others, who have chosen to delay parenthood for a few years, may bitterly regret having done so. One friend of mine who was in just this position a few years ago was incensed to be told, by a well-meaning colleague, that she ought to be pleased there weren't any children from the marriage, 'because if you meet somebody else he won't want to take the responsibility'.

In her book, *The Heart-Shaped Bullet*, the journalist Kathryn Flett writes movingly about the break-up of her marriage, which she had entered into with such high hopes, and which ended in bitter recrimination seventeen months later.

One of the reasons I had married Eric was because at some point I wanted his children and there had even been a vague plan for me to get pregnant that year, which was perhaps one of the reasons he escaped when he did. Like most women I'd fantasized about what kind of person our genetic jigsaw might create – obviously the best bits of both of us and more besides. Increasingly, then, the greatest loss seemed to be what might have been; I could feel the onset of a creeping intuition that children might not now be a part of my life. Strange, then, but though I missed so much about Eric himself, what I soon found myself missing even more was the future. I felt completely betrayed about the direction of the rest of my life.

Flett's profound sense of betrayal and rejection later led to her being hospitalised for depression. As part of her recovery from her breakdown, she wrote her book, which attempts to show why someone so apparently confident and independent could have ended up in such a state after the collapse of her marriage. If you are one of the growing numbers of couples who have chosen not to have children right away – or who have preferred to remain 'child-free' – then breaking up, as Flett suggests, may actually be even more devastating than for a couple with children.

'It felt like such a failure,' says Wendy, who works for a firm of lawyers in the City. 'After Patrick and I broke up, I kept thinking that it would have been better if we'd had a child, because then at least there'd be some tangible proof that the relationship had actually existed. As it was, people just acted as if nothing much had happened. I think they were quite surprised at work when I said I wanted to take a few days off.' While a deserted partner left at home with the children at least has their needs to distract them, the childless divorcee has no one. 'Coming home in the evenings was the worst,' recalls Wendy. 'I'd open the door to an empty house, and wonder whether it was worth bothering to cook, and all the time I'd be thinking, What's the point? If I'd had kids, at least they'd have given me a reason to go on.'

Becoming seriously depressed after her divorce, Wendy was eventually driven to seek counselling. She joined a support group for recent divorcees, changed her job, and now feels she has worked through most of the problems she encountered as a result of her marriage break-up. 'I've learned not to blame myself for what happened,' she says. 'Just because I didn't get it right first time with marriage doesn't make me a failure as a human being.'

'In some ways, getting divorced is almost harder for people who don't have kids,' says Mel, who works in publicity, and had lived with her boyfriend since both left university. 'Dave and I had lived together for nearly ten years – as long as most marriages – and yet, because we'd never got married and didn't have children, our families and even some of our friends acted as if it didn't really matter. I had friends ringing up and saying, "Never mind. I never liked him anyway..." and I'd be thinking, Hang on. This is the man I was with nine and a half years, and you're saying you never liked him? Of course I see that they were just trying to make me feel better, but it wasn't what I wanted to hear.'

Some members of Mel's family were similarly dismissive of her feelings. 'My sister's attitude was, "You were wasting your time with Dave, because he was never going to marry you" – as if I'd been hanging on for the white wedding all along. In fact it wasn't like that. Dave and I were (and still are) good friends. We'd both just changed an awful lot since we were in our early twenties. It was either stay together and have kids, or go our separate ways – which is what we decided to do. Just because we were being grown-up about it didn't mean it didn't hurt.'

Other people's insensitivity is only one of the problems encountered by childless, separating couples. Another is the feeling of having 'lost' a part of your life, which you have nothing to show for (it seems). 'I was very angry with Steve after we split up,' says Trish, who works in marketing and is now in her mid-thirties. 'I felt as if he'd "stolen" the best years of my youth. We never actually got married – he always said we didn't need a "piece of paper" to keep us together – and when we talked about having children it was always "some day". I was twenty-four when we met, and nearly thirty when we separated. During those five years, most of my friends had met "Mr Right" and settled down. I was the only one who'd ended up with nothing.'

Trish thinks the experience has made her more wary of entering into the kind of casual relationships that were a feature of her twenties. 'I've been out with people since, but I'm not prepared to get involved with anyone who's not a hundred per cent committed to me. I think "trial marriages" are a bad idea. Next time, I'm not settling for anything less than the real thing. Someone who's not interested in commitment isn't likely to interest me.'

When two people get married it is often (although not exclusively) because they intend to have children – if not immediately, then at some time in the future. The break-up of any marriage can bring with it profound feelings of failure; when the marriage is childless, these feelings are often intensified. There is no easy way out of this, and the regrets and recriminations can often last for years. If your relationship has broken up over the issue of having children, for example, it may be extremely hurtful to learn that a former partner has remarried and had a child with someone else – even though you no longer have feelings for your ex. This was the case with Maddy, whose first marriage broke up while she was in the process of establishing herself as a fashion designer.

'Don and I had both agreed that we wanted kids some day,' she now recalls. 'But we were both so busy with our careers that it never happened. When we got to the stage in our respective game plans where it would have been possible for me to take time out and get pregnant, Don always seemed to find a reason why we had to delay. Either he'd taken on too much work (he's a freelance photographer), or the flat needed doing up, or we had to

take a holiday. The baby plan was put indefinitely on hold. It was
one of the things we used to argue about a lot towards the end. I
was twenty-eight when we eventually split. A year after the
divorce, I heard that Don was living with another girl, and that
she was having his baby. I felt really sick. All those years of
stringing me along, saying we weren't "ready" to have a child,
and all the time what he meant was he didn't want to have a child
with *me*.'

Painful as such realisations may be, it is important not to let
them detract from what you, as a newly separated individual,
should be focusing on, which is not the past but the future; not
feelings of 'failure', justified or otherwise, but on what you have
yet to achieve. Other people's behaviour can be hurtful (and
nothing involves the emotions quite as much as the vexed
question of having children) but you should not dwell on this
more than absolutely necessary. Remember: you have your whole
life ahead of you to think of – goals you want to reach, people
you have yet to meet. Don't let negative emotions hold you back.

7

Dividing Up Property

When a couple split up, the bitterest arguments are often about property. It's as if the material possessions they once had in common had come to symbolise the relationship itself. Partners who have managed to be fairly civil to each other in front of children and families now find themselves at loggerheads over apparently trivial things. Possessions – especially personal ones, such as family jewellery, ornaments, books and CDs – may acquire a significance far beyond that of their actual monetary value. The dividing up of the family photo album can cause more upset, it seems, than the dividing up of the family itself. It is at this stage in the breakdown that people often decide to involve their lawyers, finding the whole unseemly business of deciding who owns what, and how much – if anything – can be salvaged from the marriage, in terms of financial assets, too much to cope with.

This is because, make no mistake, marriage is first and foremost a business contract, which, when broken by one or both parties, needs the same kind of careful handling as the dissolving of any commercial venture. And while it is perfectly possible to 'manage' your own divorce – especially if you don't have children – many separating couples find the prospect a daunting one when it comes down to the nitty-gritty of deciding what proportion of a jointly owned property such as a house or a car rightfully belongs to one or the other. Even if the split is a fairly

'You can have it on weekends and holidays, bit for the rest of the time it stays with *ME!*

The dividing up of the family photo album can cause more upset than the family itself dividing.

amicable one, it can make sense to halve legal costs by retaining one solicitor instead of two. That way, a financial settlement can be dealt with in an expert, professional way, and there isn't the risk that your straightforward, uncontentious divorce may turn into an expensive legal wrangle.

Having talked to friends who'd been through bad break-ups, I realised that the most vicious disputes were frequently over property. My friend Alexandra, locked into a bitter contest with her ex over the division of the family home and its contents, found herself resorting to petty subterfuges such as moving some of her furniture out in order to prevent him getting his hands on items she considered rightly hers. 'I'd already agreed to pay him half of what the house was worth,' she argues, with some justification. 'I was damned if I was going to let him take away half the furniture as well. It wasn't even as if the things were particularly valuable – except in a sentimental way. Mike just wanted to rub it in that he had as much "right" to them as I did, because we'd always had joint financial arrangements, so it was quite hard to work out who'd actually paid for what. I felt he was trying to humiliate me by coming into the home and taking things away that represented our life together. It was like saying to me, "Look, I'm legally entitled to do this, so I'm going to do it." He showed no sensitivity for my feelings at all.'

Paolo, another friend, recalls the day that his ex, Stevie, came round to the flat they'd shared for six years in a van she'd hired for the purpose. 'There was this bloody great pantechnicon thing parked outside and I said, "You can't be serious!" I mean, we'd agreed she could collect some of her stuff, because she and her new bloke had got this place together – but I never realised she intended taking most of our furniture,' he tells me ruefully. 'It's not even as if we were married or anything, so she had no legal entitlement to any of it. Although I wouldn't have minded her taking what she wanted – it was just the way she did it that was so cold-blooded. It was like, "I'm going to get something out of

this, even if it means trampling all over someone else's feelings."
I felt she did it deliberately to hurt me.'

Even when the process of dividing up possessions has been
agreeably worked out in advance, it can still be extremely painful.
Watching favourite items of clothing, books, CDs and ornaments
being packed into 'Yours' and 'Mine' boxes is like watching your
past being dismantled in front of your eyes. Inevitably, objects
have memories attached to them, so that even things that have very
little material value in themselves – that scratchy old Aretha
Franklin LP he found for you in the bargain bin in Cheapo
Records; the holey old sweater he always wore on Saturdays
because you gave it to him – can unleash a rush of associations.
'The funny thing was,' says Kate, recalling her own experience of
this, 'I'd hardly cried at all until the day Sean came back to the flat
to get his things. Then it was as if the floodgates were opened. I
just sat in the middle of the living room with all these boxes on the
floor around me, howling my eyes out. I think it was only then,
when I saw him packing up his books and records and stuff, that it
hit me that it was really all over between us.'

Arguing over who gets to keep the wedding presents may seem
a trivial thing to get upset about, compared with the larger fact of
divorce and separation itself. But in fact it may be symbolic of a
whole range of other disputes. Suddenly, all the suppressed rage
and tension that has led up to this moment – the dividing up of
household goods – can surface, to devastating effect. 'I couldn't
believe how mean-minded Patrick was when it came to sorting
out his things from mine,' says Wendy. 'He actually drew up a
list, with different headings – "Towels", "Crockery", "Kitchen
Utensils", that kind of thing. He was so set on this idea that he
was entitled to half of everything that it was as if he had no room
to spare for how it would make me feel. In a way, it seemed to
stand for all the bad aspects of the relationship. I can remember
standing there quite calmly while he went around the flat ticking
things off his list, and thinking, Thank God it's over. How on

earth did I stay with this creep for so long? It was quite therapeutic, I guess.'

'We had our biggest rows over who got to keep what,' recalls Jen. 'There was a gold watch which had been my father's, which I'd given to Matt one Christmas. He said he wanted to keep it, but I said, "No way." It wasn't that it was particularly valuable or anything, but it meant a lot to me. The idea that he might get to keep something which had once belonged to someone I loved was unbearable. In the end, he caved in. But it made things quite unpleasant for a while, with Matt saying that, if he had to give back my dad's watch, then he wanted me to return my engagement ring. It got very petty. But I suppose divorce is like that.'

Divorce, sadly is all too often 'like that', when couples cannot agree over the division of jointly owned property. It is often then that things have to go to court, with both parties standing to incur expensive legal costs in order to resolve the situation. This is most obviously the case when a large item, such as a house or flat, is in dispute. In this instance, the law is fairly clear-cut, especially where the property is in the name of both partners. Then, the various options open to the court are: to transfer one spouse's interest in the property to the other (usually with a lump-sum adjustment, to compensate the partner whose interest is being given up); to order that the property should be sold, and the proceeds jointly divided; to order an outright transfer (without compensation) from one spouse to the other; and to order a postponed sale (usually after any children of the marriage have completed their education). However, there are no hard-and-fast rules about this, and most judges have fairly wide discretionary powers when it comes to divorce cases. Selling the property and dividing the proceeds 50:50 may be appropriate in certain cases, where the marriage has been short and there are no children; in many others, it would be downright unfair! The court's decision will depend entirely on whether or not there are children involved, whether the spouse who is moving out of the family home has secure accommodation or not, the length of the marriage and many other factors.

In a case where the property is not jointly owned, the partner whose name is not on the title deeds still has some legal rights, which can be safeguarded by the courts. These include: the right not to be evicted without a court order if he or she is in occupation; the right (if the court thinks fit) of him or her to return to the marital home if he or she has left it; and the right (again, if the court thinks it appropriate) to exclude the owner spouse from the home for a period (usually only when violence has occurred). It is worth bearing these facts in mind if, like many people who find themselves in the middle of divorce proceedings, you are unsure of your legal position. Nothing is worse, for anyone going through the emotional traumas of separation, than to feel that your home may suddenly be taken away from you. For anyone in this position, the most sensible option is to consult a lawyer as soon as possible. Those in financial difficulties should take the first step of applying for Legal Aid. One thing to bear in mind is that, whether you jointly own your family home or not, the court's priority is always first and foremost to consider the interests of any children of the marriage, and to ensure that, whatever happens, there is an adequate home for them.

Quite apart from any problems that may arise over the division of property, another all too common cause of friction between separating couples is over the question of finance. For some couples, arguments over money may be a contributory factor in the breakdown of the marriage; for others, disputes over finance may only start with the divorce proceedings themselves, as each partner tries to get as good a deal as possible from the eventual settlement. Still other couples may find that their financial troubles begin some time after the divorce, with one spouse (usually but not exclusively the husband) becoming increasingly reluctant to make regular financial payments towards the family's upkeep, and the other (frequently but not always the wife) finding herself impoverished as a result.

Caroline, now in her late forties with four children in their teens, found herself badly hit by a post-divorce reduction of income, when her husband Mark, a company director, left her for his secretary, Debra. From having been a full-time housewife and mother, with a comfortable lifestyle, she was forced to take a part-time job in order to keep up the mortgage payments on the family home, after Mark's business failed and he became unable to meet the substantial payments stipulated in the divorce settlement. 'It was bad enough in the early days after he left,' she remembers, 'because suddenly I was having to manage on a fixed income. It sounded quite a generous amount on paper, but when everything was taken into consideration – the mortgage and the children's school fees and so on – it dwindled away to nothing quite quickly each month. There was certainly no "extra" for treats, as there had been when we were married.

'The first year after the divorce I couldn't even afford to take a holiday. When Mark was declared bankrupt, things went from bad to worse. The maintenance payments were cut in half, and then dried up altogether. It wasn't any use putting pressure on him through the Child Support Agency, because there just wasn't the money there to give me. It was all tied up in the bankruptcy proceedings. In fact, the only good thing to come out of the whole awful mess was that, at an earlier stage in the divorce, the house had been transferred into my name. That meant, at least, that it couldn't be sequestered by the courts as an asset. Otherwise the children and I might have found ourselves on the streets!

'We had some very bad months when it looked as if I might have to sell the house. Amanda, our eldest, was just about to do her GCSEs, and it would have been terrible if she'd had to change schools. Fortunately, the school was very understanding and agreed to waive the fees for a few months until things got straight. The building society reduced my mortgage temporarily to an "interest-only" payment. And then Martin, a family friend who's a solicitor, suggested I should go and work for him for a time. My secretarial skills were a bit rusty but I was just glad to be doing something to sort out the mess we'd got ourselves into. It was quite frightening, really.

'Even though I know it wasn't as a direct consequence of the divorce, I still blame Mark for what had happened. If he hadn't decided to have an affair, we might still have been together, and we could have pooled our efforts to sort out the overall financial problem. As it was, we were pulling against each other – and life became very bloody indeed.'

It isn't always the abandoned wife who comes off worse, where a financial settlement is involved. Stephen, the owner of a company selling computer components, found himself under considerable pressure from his ex to increase her monthly maintenance payments, after the company was floated on the stock market. 'Felicity was quite unscrupulous in using the children to get what she wanted from me. Even though it was over two years since we'd parted, she was determined to get her pound of flesh. Letters used to arrive from the lawyers every couple of weeks, making increasingly unreasonable demands. I was already paying two sets of school fees, but she'd add in the cost of an entire new school uniform – which it later transpired had never been bought.

'Then it was expensive holidays – skiing trips and the like – which she said the girls needed in order to keep up with their friends. If I questioned any of these amounts, she'd threaten to take me to court, and stop me seeing my daughters at all. The only way to get her off my back was to give her more money.'

The situation got so bad that Stephen and his ex-wife did end up in court, after Felicity petitioned to have her maintenance payments increased in line with Stephen's increased income from his business. 'She thought she was being very clever, getting it all down in black and white – but the net result was that she actually ended up getting less than I'd been giving her over the previous two years. When you added in all the extras – holidays and riding lessons for the girls and so on – it had amounted to more than the actual amount we'd agreed in the divorce settlement. The judge was quite sympathetic to my case, in fact, because by then Felicity was living with someone else and money wasn't a problem at all, whereas I was still working like stink to keep the business afloat and maintain two households. So, in the end, Felicity got her increased payments – but I also got regular access to the girls, which she'd been trying to deny me. So you could say it ended in a draw.'

Such adversarial contests are all too often a feature of divorce, especially where money is concerned. Fuelled by stories in the press about the large sums awarded to high-profile divorcees such as Ivana Trump and Jerry Hall, this take-him-to-the-cleaner's mentality has become widespread in recent years, with the emphasis on 'punishing' the errant spouse by hitting him (or her) where it hurts – in the pocket. While such an attitude is not hard to understand, it may have unwelcome consequences, as the relationship between former partners degenerates into a slanging match. Far better for everyone concerned – in particular the children of the relationship – is when a couple decide to use mediation to settle all the issues involved in separation.

Dividing the finance and property

Even when the divorce procedure itself is fairly straightforward, the finance and property aspects can drag on for ages, producing seemingly endless affidavits, and causing much bitterness, as couples fight over who owns what and how much each feels they have a right to. So it is worth keeping a sense of proportion about this issue, and remembering that there is only a finite amount of money and property to divide.

Is it worth getting into a huge fight over what might be relatively insignificant sums, in order to prove a point? Obviously, if you feel you have been hard done by, you should enlist the services of a lawyer to fight your corner. But remember, some of the resentment you may be feeling towards your former partner is resentment at the thought of someone else – a judge or solicitor – dictating how 'your' money should be divided and how best it should be made use of, when what you want right now is to be financially independent.

Finance and property: some do's and don'ts

- **Do** keep accurate financial records of income, expenditure, and debts. For example, make sure you have your P60, which details your income in the previous tax year. An affidavit can be much more effective if backed up by the appropriate documents.

- **Do** check your tax position with your accountant or solicitor, or with the Inland Revenue. Paying or being in receipt of maintenance can affect your tax position a great deal. You may find, if you are paying maintenance, that you will have to pay much less tax – but only if the maintenance is the result of a court order or Child Support Agency assessment. Voluntary payments will not affect your tax position.

- **Do** recognise that dependent children can make a considerable difference to a financial and property agreement. The parent who looks after the children has a good claim to financial provision for this.

- **Do** remember that there are no set rates for maintenance for ex-spouses. This can cause wide variations in payments to ex-spouses, as the court has to take into account disposable income in each case.

- **Don't** be rushed into accepting a low offer in a financial or property settlement on the grounds that 'it will be better than nothing'. Having accepted a low offer in the first place, it will be harder to get a court to accept your request for an increase in the future. Be realistic about your needs!

- **Don't** forget that divorce affects inheritance (except in Scotland or Northern Ireland). When a divorce takes place, an ex-spouse who would have benefited is seen in the eyes of the law as having died on the day before the divorce! Children, however, remain eligible for a share in the estate. Make sure your will is up to date!

The Child Support Agency

Set up in 1993, the CSA was intended to deal with child-maintenance arrangements – previously set up by the court and by the Department of Social Security (DSS) – by calculating maintenance according to parents' income, and enforcing its payment by the absent parent (often the father). Although its aims were laudable, in that it attempted to reduce the number of parents defaulting on their maintenance payments, and thus reduce child poverty, its methods have been widely criticised and have – some allege – increased, rather than decreased, the bitterness of maintenance battles.

Who is eligible for child maintenance?

- Parents who have been separated can apply any time after the separation. You do not need to be divorced first.
- Claims can be made only for natural or adopted children, not stepchildren.
- Both parents and child must be resident in the UK.
- Children must be under sixteen, or nineteen if still in full-time education.

How do I apply?

You can apply through your local DSS office, or call the CSA Enquiry Line (see Useful Organisations).

What is family mediation?

Family mediation is a process in which trained and impartial mediators assist those involved in a relationship breakdown to reach some areas of common agreement. The issues discussed may concern the relationship itself, or may focus on more practical matters such as finance, property and visiting rights. Mediators can help you resolve together:

- whether your marriage is over
- arrangements for the children
- financial arrangements for the future
- what to do about the family home
- any other matters relating to your family situation

While it is not an alternative to legal advice, it does mean you do not necessarily have to engage solicitors to act on your behalf. Instead, you and your former partner try to work things out face to face, with a third party to negotiate between you and to help resolve areas of conflict. Unlike marriage guidance, in which the emphasis is on relationships and feelings, family mediation is concerned with the practical issues that divorce involves. While it may not be right for everybody, it does provide an alternative to the sometimes adversarial approach adopted by the courts, with resulting reduction of stress for both sides.

Tim and Rachel were among the thousands of people each year to seek family mediation, when their marriage broke up as a result of Tim's infidelity. 'We were getting on really badly after Rachel found out about Helen. The stupid thing was, I'd already broken the affair off by then – but Rachel felt she could never forgive me. She told me she wanted a divorce, but, when we tried to discuss the details of what that would mean for ourselves and the kids, we always ended up shouting at each other. Then a friend at work suggested counselling, and put me in touch with the National Family Mediation network, who gave me an address in our area. When I told Rachel, she wasn't very happy at first, because one of her hang-ups is she can't bear the idea of discussing her problems with strangers – but later she agreed to give it a try.

'Our first meeting wasn't a great success. Rachel arrived in a very negative mood, determined to have her say about how badly I'd treated her. I'd naïvely thought we might have been able to move on from that, to a discussion of what we were going to do about the children's future. In the end, we compromised – with the mediator's help – and talked about what we both wanted from each other and from the separation. It took quite a number of further meetings before we established an agenda we could discuss calmly – but it did eventually happen. The presence of a third party means you don't get quite so heated. If the conversation did start to get angry, our mediator used to allocate each of us a set time in which to have our say, before letting the other person reply, also without interruption. It was a good technique.'

The mediation process has a set structure, which breaks down into five stages:

- engaging the couple into the mediation process
- establishing the agenda by identifying the issues to be discussed
- exploring the issues by discussing the facts fully
- generating options by thinking of different ways of resolving issues
- reaching agreement by choosing options that best suit both parties

At the end of the mediation process, if all the options have been successfully worked out, a written agreement may be drawn up, to help the couple stick to what they have agreed. 'I found it immensely helpful in resolving my difficulties with Rachel. It was good therapy, voicing some of the things we resented about the other person's behaviour, without it turning into a name-calling session. And it was useful talking over what we both wanted for ourselves and for the children,' says Tim. 'That was what helped us both through – the knowledge that, deep down, we both wanted the best for Poppy and Jack.'

Sorting out arrangements to do with property and possessions is important, both from a practical point of view – you and your former partner need to have somewhere to live – and from an emotional perspective. The family home – whether this is a six-bedroom mansion or a one-bedroom flat – symbolises security, to most of us. When this is threatened, by the departure of one partner, or the infidelity of another, people feel destabilised and defensive. Often, a property may have to be sold, following a divorce, to meet legal costs or to fit a reduced income. This in itself can feel like a terrible blow.

Again, it is crucial not to panic – and to keep in mind certain things. These are: that people are always more important than property; that financial problems, however grim, can be overcome more easily than health problems – so that it isn't worth making yourself ill worrying about them; and that change, however painful, is not always something to be feared.

8

'Two Families Are Better Than One'

Divorce – which obviously pulls families apart – can also, paradoxically, be something that brings them together. Even though it is all too common for families of separating partners to 'take sides' and apportion blame (sometimes unfairly) for what has happened, it is also not unusual for parents and in-laws to try to hold the remaining structures of the family together, as far as possible. For grandparents especially, who fear losing contact with beloved grandchildren, mending fences with a son or daughter-in-law can seem of paramount importance.

'Phil's parents and I didn't actually get on all that well when we were married,' recalls Cassie, a journalist in her mid-thirties, with three young children. 'My mother-in-law was particularly critical – always finding fault with the way I did things for the children. I resented their constant interference in our lives, and the fact that Phil could never say no to them about every little thing. It caused quite a lot of friction between us – in fact, on several occasions, Phil accused me of "hating" his parents! The weird thing is that, now we've split up, Mary and Joe couldn't be sweeter towards me. They're always offering to take the kids off my hands, so that I can have odd weekends to myself, and Mary, my mother-in-law, has gone out of her way to say how much she values me as an "adopted daughter". I think they were afraid that, when Phil and I broke up, they'd miss out on seeing the children.

Of course I would never want that to happen. Kids need grandparents.'

While it is tempting (and often understandable) to 'blame' your partner's family when you are going through a divorce, it is something to be avoided if you want to establish a good working relationship with your children's grandparents and uncles and aunts in the aftermath of the break-up. The reasons for this are two-fold. First, it is more than likely that, whatever your feelings towards your former in-laws might be, your ex-partner will continue to visit them with the children from time to time, and so it makes sense for that contact to be as stress-free as possible. If you make your dislike of your ex's family obvious to your children, that is going to create further confusion and anxiety about divided loyalties in their minds. Secondly, you yourself may occasionally (at Christmas, or on the children's birthdays, say) have to get in touch with them. If you start off on a hostile footing, it makes even the simplest contacts fraught with tension.

The great thing to remember is that it is your children's sense of wellbeing that is the most important thing. Maintaining the relationships they have with their grandparents and other relatives is a way of reinforcing their feelings of stability. It is quite painful enough to 'lose' a parent through divorce; losing half your family on top of that is more than any child should have to cope with. Even where there is bad feeling between you and your in-laws, this ought not to affect the way you all behave in front of the kids. And sometimes your ex-in-laws may prove an unexpected support in time of crisis. They can offer everything from practical help with holiday arrangements to financial help with school fees or expenses. If you keep the lines of communication open from the start, there is more chance that the relationship will develop into something new – a positive and loving bond between you, your kids and their 'other family'. Which can only be a beneficial thing, for all concerned.

'I'd always had a very good relationship with my in-laws even before the break-up,' says Emma. 'In fact, they were almost more angry with Martin over what he'd done to our marriage than I was. I think the fact that I was the "innocent" one in the affair meant that they automatically took my side. Plus they were absolutely devoted to Rosie and Grace. There was no way they were going to give up being grandparents, just because Martin had given up on being a father.'

So indignant did Martin's parents, Eve and Jack, feel at the way their son had treated Emma that they at first refused to meet his new girlfriend, Lauren. 'They'd arrange for him to visit them with the children, and then he'd let slip he was bringing her as well, and they'd say, "In that case, we'll go and see them at Emma's",' recalls their former daughter-in-law. 'It got to the situation where I was acting as the peacemaker between Martin and his own parents! And in the end we sorted something out, for Rosie and Grace's sake.'

The arrangement they eventually worked out was that Martin and Lauren could drop the girls off with their grandparents for the weekend, and then pick them up afterwards, but that Emma, when she took her daughters to visit, would stay the night. 'They were very concerned about my feelings, which I found quite touching,' says Emma. 'It was as if they were constantly trying to reassure me that they still cared about me, and the relationship we'd had.'

While the early months of break-up can be fraught with such conflicts of loyalty, eventually there may come a time when you and your ex – to say nothing of your children, and parents and in-laws – will have to accept that things have now changed irrevocably. You and your former partner may both be in new relationships, with other partners and even other children. It is time to move on, and make the best of the new situation, rather than try to cling on to what is now in the past. It is at this stage – a year, two years or maybe more after the divorce itself – that the process of reconstruction begins, as far as you and your children are concerned. Achieving a fair and amicable divorce requires both partners to establish a relationship that will serve as a basis for continuing to meet your responsibilities as parents. If your children come to feel at home in both of your homes, you will have achieved a great deal. If they feel comfortable about moving from one to the other without fear of upsetting you or your ex-partner by doing so, you will also be doing well. And, if you have energy and confidence to begin the next phase of your life with or without a new partner, you will have avoided the worst effects of divorce and – more importantly – *saved your children* from the worst effects of divorce. After all, it is their lives and their futures that come first.

Creating an extended family doesn't happen overnight, but happen it certainly does, if you are prepared to let it. Suddenly, as well as existing family structures, there are a whole range of new ones. This is one of the things that distinguish our society from all those that have come before it – its willingness to embrace change, and to redefine the role of the family. In practical terms, this may mean that your children will have two homes instead of one. They will have new roles within those families, and perhaps end up seeing themselves and their own lives rather differently from the way they did before.

'It was funny when my dad decided to get married again,' says Natasha, recalling her parents' divorce when she was in her teens. 'Because up to that point I'd been the "baby" of the family. Hearing that Davina, my father's new wife, was pregnant threw me a bit – although I was also quite excited by the prospect of having a new baby brother or sister. But it was as if I'd suddenly grown up. I wasn't this little girl any longer. Maybe if my mum had been less cool about the whole thing, I'd have handled it less well.'

Not all children of a divorcing couple are able to treat their mother or father's new partner in such a matter-of-fact way. In fact – as fictional accounts such as Joanna Trollope's marvellously astute drama about divorce, *Other People's*

Children, show only too clearly – many children have a great deal of difficulty dealing with the whole idea of their parent being involved with someone new. Even children who have handled the fact of the divorce itself reasonably well may find themselves thrown by the realisation that their mother or father has formed a new allegiance, which may or may not include them.

'It was our middle child, Luke, who reacted the worst when Josh and I got together,' recalls Teresa. 'He'd been very cut up about the separation itself, and very angry with Richard about his treatment of me. Boys can be quite protective towards their mothers, and Luke was at a vulnerable age – just turned fifteen. I suppose it was naïve to think he'd be altogether happy about my seeing somebody else.'

Luke's response when Josh started spending occasional nights at the family home was to cut off communication altogether. 'Basically, he retreated into himself,' Teresa recalls. 'From being a bright, outgoing child, he became moody, sarcastic and aggressive. He wouldn't answer when spoken to, and started taking food up to his room when he wanted to eat, instead of sitting down with the rest of us for meals. Eventually it got so bad that my relationship with Josh was starting to suffer. I felt I was sacrificing Luke's welfare for my own selfish reasons, and even seriously considered ending the relationship.'

Feeling guilty when your relationship with your child's father breaks down, or when you start a new relationship with someone else, is a common experience for people who have been through a divorce. In Teresa's case, it was complicated by the fact that she was not divorced from Richard, her children's father, at the time she became involved with Josh, her lover. 'I suppose subconsciously Luke must have felt I might still get back together again with Richard,' she says. 'When Josh appeared on the scene, he realised that wasn't going to happen.'

Over the next few months, Teresa worked hard at making her son feel better about the fact that his parents were no longer together. 'I tried to spend as much time with him as I could, and talk to him about all sorts of issues – not just the separation. Luke's a very sensitive and thoughtful boy. I think he just felt no one had bothered to consider *his* feelings very much. Fortunately, because I was still on such good terms with Richard, I was able to enlist his help in talking to Luke about the situation. Sometimes it's easier for a father to discuss those kinds of things with a son than for a mother. And Josh and I tried to be as discreet as possible about our relationship, because we knew Luke found it hard to handle. The funny thing is, they now get on really well. It wasn't Josh himself Luke disliked – just the idea of him.'

For teenage children, particularly, it may be difficult to cope with the idea that their parents have a sex life. This is even a problem for children whose parents are still married – so it is all the more so when a new partner is involved. Again, sensitivity is the key. Your child may be hostile and aggressive towards you or your new love – but remember, he or she *is* just a child. You are the one who has to be 'grown up' about the situation. Encourage your child to talk about what is bothering them. If they can't – or won't – say, then try to express the situation as simply and clearly as you can, showing that you have taken their feelings into consideration. Say something like, 'I know you're finding it awkward having somebody else in the house, but you must see that I have to have friendships too.' Suggest ways in which the situation might be made more bearable for everyone. You could say, 'Since we've all got to get along together, it might make sense if we had a few ground rules. So, if you can try to be polite to X, then X and I will stay out of the TV room when you have your friends around on Saturday nights.' Making small concessions isn't a sign that you're 'giving in'. The more reasonable your demands (basic politeness, doing a share of the household chores), the more your child will see that you haven't stopped caring about him or her just because there's someone else in your life.

Children of an earlier relationship can often end up getting on very well with a parent's 'new' partner, who may be able to offer advice and support that is relatively free from emotional involvement. Leah, whose parents divorced when she was thirteen, gets on well with both step-parents, whom she has come to regard as family – rather like additional uncles and aunts, or older siblings. 'My dad moved out to live with someone else when I was quite young, so I've had over ten years to get used to the fact that my parents aren't together, and to adapt to the idea that they've both got somebody else. It wasn't always as easy in the early days! To begin with, my brother and I really resented our dad's girlfriend, Felicity – mainly because we blamed her for the divorce. Actually, my mother's told me more recently that it was *she* who asked my father to leave. But when you're a kid you tend to see things in a very simplified way. So we made Felicity's life a bit of a misery at first. When we used to visit, we'd refuse to eat anything she cooked, and be really cheeky to her when my Dad wasn't around – stuff like that.

'Then, one day, about a year after my parents divorced, I was spending the weekend at my dad's and Felicity came and knocked on the door of my bedroom and asked if she could speak to me. She said my dad had asked her to marry him, but that she didn't want to give him an answer until she'd asked me what I thought, because if it was going to make me very unhappy, then she'd tell my dad the answer was no. But that she really loved my dad, and she cared very much for me and Richard, and that if we could see our way to accepting her she'd love to be part of our family. I think it was the first time anyone had ever asked my advice about anything so important, and I was just bowled over. I don't know exactly what I said, but I remember things got a lot better from then on. My dad and Felicity did eventually get married. Now I regard her as just another member of the family – like a big sister, really.'

When Leah was going through the 'difficult' teens, wearing

outrageous clothes and indulging in provocative behaviour at home and school, her stepmother often acted as a 'buffer' between her and the authorities, she recalls. 'There was one time I was in real trouble at school. I'd been cheeky to one of the teachers, and then failed to turn up for a detention. They were talking about suspending me. Felicity was the one who went up to the school on my behalf and calmed the whole thing down. She was also really great when my dad used to nag me about the clothes I wore, or what time I was supposed to be in after parties. She said she could remember what it was like, being young and wanting your freedom, and feeling that nobody understood you – so it was an advantage for me to have her on my side. It may sound a funny thing to say,' says Leah – now settled into her first job, and happily living with a boyfriend – 'but I think of Felicity as one of my best friends.'

Being part of an extended family can have its downside, but at its best, it can offer a whole range of new and potentially rewarding relationships. And, while it is seldom easy for children of a pre-existing relationship to accept a parent's new partner, this can be achieved over time, and can end up being of lasting value to both stepchild and step-parent. While tales of wicked stepmothers and nasty stepchildren are all common, even nowadays, it is heartening to know that, for some people at least, the extended-families idea can actually work. And if you can make it work – by being accepting towards your ex's new partner, for example, instead of behaving with hostility – then the healing process of getting over a divorce will be accelerated.

Contact and parental responsibility

Before the 1989 Children Act, an absent parent's visiting rights were referred to as 'access'; now the term 'contact' is used to describe the regular pattern of visits a parent may need – and a court may prescribe – to maintain a relationship with his or her child. If you are the parent who has left the family home, then you will have applied for a court order – called a **contact order** – specifying the amount of contact or visiting time you may have with your child. If you are the full-time parent with whom the child is living, then a **residence order** will have been made by the court to put this arrangement in place. Either way, your role will bring with it certain responsibilities.

If you are the 'absent' (i.e. nonresidential) parent, then you will have had to adjust to a very great change in your relationship with your children, and with your former partner. This may seem so obvious as not to need stating, but the fact is, many families have terrible difficulty getting used to it. Instead of having their father (or mother) at home with them all or most of the time, children have to get used to the idea that Dad (or Mum) is no longer just a 'part of the furniture', whom they can take for granted, or not, as they please, but someone whom they see only on 'special' occasions – at weekends, birthdays and Christmas, for example. This can cause considerable tension – both on the part of the children themselves, who may be unsettled by the disruption to their lives, and on the part of the parent, forced into the role of part-time mother or father, with all its accompanying awkwardness.

'From having been a really "hands-on" sort of father, always helping the kids with their homework and playing football in the park and stuff, suddenly I was this useless individual who turned up on alternate weekends,' recalls Simon, whose marriage to Andrea ended in divorce eight years ago. 'It was OK at first, because I did that thing that all absent fathers do, which is to spoil the kids rotten. Always taking them to McDonald's and stuffing them with sweets – that was me! But then Andrea started sending me these angry little notes, telling me not to keep buying them things. There was one week, I think, I bought the boys skateboards, which she'd been saving up to buy for their birthdays. After that particular falling-out, I tried a bit harder to see things her way. But it was difficult, only seeing the boys every other week. I felt they might forget me – or not love me any more – if I didn't buy them everything they wanted.'

For some parents (and children) visiting times can turn into an ordeal precisely because the parent tries too hard – as Simon did – to make things 'special'. Kids like things to be relaxed and normal, not 'different' or strange. Where possible, try to establish a routine for them, rather than overload them with too many 'treats' and too much excitement. A quiet afternoon watching television at home with Dad, or a trip to the local supermarket to buy food for supper, can be a lot more enjoyable for a child than any amount of expensive outings or unnecessary presents.

'Things got much better after I moved into my new flat,' says Simon. 'It's not huge, but it was somewhere I could bring them on the afternoons it was my turn to have them. When I bought the place, I made sure there was a spare room, so that, if Jake or Georgie wanted to stay over, they could. We still go places together – especially since they've both started supporting my football team! – and I still buy them things occasionally (with Andrea's agreement). But it's all a lot more settled and normal for us all.'

If you are the 'full-time' parent, then having established visiting times can provide a welcome respite, after a week or more of coping alone. If you know your children are safe and happy, you can relax, and enjoy some 'me-time' of your own. Of course, it isn't always as simple or straightforward as that; even for the full-time mum or dad, visiting times can be fraught with tension.

'It used to be hell,' recalls Marianne, of the period immediately after her divorce from Lucas. 'Our kids were just at the wrong age – ten and thirteen – and they really let their resentment show of the way things had changed. Lucas would arrive to collect them for the weekend and Colette – that's my eldest – would be still in bed, having refused to pack her things or get dressed, or eat her breakfast. That used to upset Janine, the little one, so then *she'd* refuse to go. And then I'd get upset, because Lucas would be sitting in the kitchen, muttering about how he didn't know why he bothered, because everyone hated him anyway, and he might as well give up and go home – and I'd be frantically trying to get the girls moving, because I wanted to get to my art class or go shopping or whatever. It was a nightmare.'

After talking to Colette, her thirteen-year-old, Marianne discovered that the cause of the problem was her daughter's embarrassment at seeing their father with another woman. 'They were at a very sensitive age where sex was concerned – especially Colette. Seeing Lucas – who's a very physical man – hugging and kissing his girlfriend was embarrassing for them. Also, they both felt that spending time with Emily was a kind of disloyalty to me. So we came to an arrangement that, on the weekends the children visited, Emily would pop in for tea or take them shopping or something, but not stay the night. She was quite good about that. It helped get the girls used to having her around, without making them feel threatened by the arrangement. And it meant I got my weekends – which I needed!'

What to do if one or all of the children do not want to go

- **They may feel guilty** about leaving the parent they live with to visit the other parent. They may see this as a betrayal – a feeling reinforced if the 'full-time' parent says things like, 'I'll be lonely when you're gone', or makes them feel they shouldn't enjoy being with the other parent as much. Try to resist the temptation to do this.
- **They may have other things to do** that may create a conflict. Kids have busy social lives these days. Fitting in regular

Some divorced parents use their children as 'go-betweens'.

contact visits with all the other demands they have on their time – from birthday parties to school trips – can create conflict. After all, if you had to cancel every weekend when *you* had something planned with your friends to go on a family visit, you'd be resentful. Try to be flexible.

- **They may feel bored.** Sometimes, the last thing kids want is to be dragged off to a museum, or forced to go and stay with grandparents. It's no good resorting to the 'when I was your age' argument. Instead, encourage them to say what *they* want to do with the time. You never know – they may come up with some good ideas!

- **They may hate being asked questions** about the other parent. Some divorced parents use their children as 'go-betweens' in a war of nerves, endlessly grilling them about what 'his' new girlfriend is like, or how much 'she' spends on going to the hairdresser's each week. Don't do this. It isn't fair to your children and it only prolongs the resentment between you and your ex. If you want to ask your ex something, pick up the telephone.

One way or another, you – and your ex – will have to come to a working arrangement concerning your children, that is, if you both want the parent–child relationship to continue. And, despite the many pitfalls inherent in the situation, some of which are referred to above, there are many good reasons for doing this. The first, and most important, is that, even if you no longer live with your children, they *are* still your children, and they still need your love and care. The second, almost as important, is that *you* need them. Even if your relationship with your ex is over, your relationship with your children is still something to treasure.

9
Joining the Singletons

If you have just come out of a long-term relationship, adjusting to being on your own can seem daunting. Suddenly, instead of facing the world as part of a 'team', you have to face it as an individual. Instead of taking refuge in the mutual reassurances of coupledom, you're out on your own. It's exciting – but it can also seem intimidating. And as with a bereavement, the recovery process can take a long time – sometimes as much as two years. Psychologists' studies have shown that, broadly speaking, most break-ups follow a recognisable pattern – starting with the disillusionment that occurs when a couple are on the brink of splitting up, and going through successive stages of estrangement before the break-up itself. Even after the actual physical separation, there are further stages you may find yourself going through, before you feel ready for a new relationship. A period of 'mourning' – for your marriage, and for the person you once were before your divorce – may be one of these.

'There were just so many practicalities to deal with,' recalls Kate, of the period following her divorce from Sean. 'And I had Liam to think of, as well as coping with work. When you run your own company, you simply can't afford to take time out – even if you're falling apart inside. I don't think I let myself grieve about what had happened between me and Sean for a long time. It was just "business as usual" for me – at least on the surface. Of course, underneath I was feeling terrible: furious with Sean for letting me down the way he did, but also furious with myself for letting it happen. I remember one day, about a year after I split up with Sean, leaving work early so that I could pick up Liam from nursery to take him to his swimming class, and getting stuck in a traffic jam on the way and knowing I was going to be late and bursting into tears. Afterwards I felt like such a fool, sitting there with tears pouring down my face, banging my fists up and down on the steering wheel and screaming "No, no, no!" But I suppose it all had to come out, sooner or later.'

Kate's way of coping with the grief of ending her marriage was characteristic, she now admits. 'I immersed myself in work. It seemed the only thing which was going to keep me sane. Because I run my own company, there was no one to say to me, "Kate, you've had enough. Go home." I just kept on working longer and longer hours, trying to channel some of the anger I was feeling into something positive. In the end I made myself ill.' Through a combination of overwork and skipping meals, Kate lost a stone and a half, and concerned friends began to notice she was a mere shadow of her former self.

'I think maybe subconsciously I was punishing myself for the divorce,' she reflects. 'It was as if I felt I deserved to suffer, just because I'd lost Sean.' The turning point came when a friend of Kate's returned from Canada and they met for a drink. 'Erin told me I was much too thin – "gaunt" was the word she used – and that if I didn't stop working flat out I'd give myself a nervous breakdown. I suppose I just needed someone to tell me to sort myself out.'

Like many other young professional women, Kate had a network of friends she could turn to when the going got tough – friends who were roughly her own age, and who'd had similar experiences they could draw on to help her through her difficulties. 'All my friends were brilliant while I was going through the divorce – ringing me up at odd times for a chat, and that sort of thing. But Erin was the best – maybe because she'd been through a bad break-up herself not too long before. She was always "there" for me – offering lots of practical help, as well as emotional support. For my birthday, she booked me a day at the Sanctuary [a spa in London], and even looked after Liam for me when I went. She was also the sort of person you could ring up if you were feeling miserable and needed to talk, without having to apologise or make excuses.'

Having a support network of friends and close family members is invaluable in the aftermath of break-up. Knowing that you can call on people when you need them – whether it's for a late-night chat or to have someone to go to the gym with – can be a great relief when things are looking bleak. 'It sounds a really weird thing to say, but I never realised how many friends I had until I got divorced,' says Sarah. 'When Ian and I were together, we tended to see other friends who were also in couples. After we separated, my women friends really came into their own. I'd lived in the area over ten years, so there was quite a big group of us – women my age (late thirties), who'd had their children around the same time as I had mine, and who'd had similar experiences. Not all of them were single, of course – although there was one friend who'd also been through a recent divorce. She and I would compare notes about how we were coping with the pressures of being single again, and occasionally we'd arrange a girls' night out together, and have a good bitch about our exes. But my married friends were equally supportive. It was just great to be able to drop round if I was feeling a bit sorry for myself, and have a drink and a natter. I think I got much closer to my friends during the period immediately after the divorce, than I had been before.'

'My girlfriends were great,' recalls Trish. 'I don't know how I'd have survived the break-up with Steve without them. I was lucky, because I had this really lovely group of mates from college whom I'd never stopped seeing, even after I was married, so they were all there for me when things started to get tough. My best friend, Sasha, still lives in Manchester, where we were at university together, and when I phoned her to tell her the news about me and Steve she said, "Right. You're getting a train and coming up here for the weekend." We had the most fantastic time, going out drinking in all our old haunts, and talking things over, that it really made me feel a whole lot better. Sometimes the worst thing about going through a bad time is feeling that nobody cares. With Sasha and my other friends, I always had someone to turn to.'

Coming through the emotional firestorms of divorce and separation can be exhausting, physically and mentally. It can leave you feeling vulnerable and shaken, with your self-esteem at an all-time low. Even if your partner has not left you for someone else, it is hard to escape feelings of rejection and failure, and fears that no one will ever want to be with you again. Often, these self-doubting, self-hating feelings can result in a neglect of one's health. 'Comfort' eating or not bothering to eat at all are ways in which newly separated people can express their unhappiness – ending up in a vicious circle of weight gain or weight loss, which (apart from being dangerous if carried to extremes) is a physical sign that the person concerned doesn't care about him- or herself.

'I just lost interest in everything,' says Wendy. 'Eating was too much trouble. Getting my hair done was too much trouble. Seeing friends was too much trouble. If I couldn't have Patrick, I didn't want to go on. It all seemed like too much of an effort.' Wendy's high-stress job as a family lawyer meant she was all the more vulnerable to emotional pressures. 'I'd come home from work feeling like a limp rag. Having to deal with the details of other people's break-ups and custody battles was almost more than I could bear. In the end, I just wasn't doing my job properly, because my mind was on my own problems.'

Fortunately for Wendy, a colleague at work to whom she'd confided the news of her separation was concerned enough to suggest she should take a break. 'I had some leave pending, which meant I could hand over the cases I was working on to someone else in the office. It was either that or have a nervous breakdown. And having those few weeks to sort myself out made a huge difference. By the time I returned to work, I felt I was back in charge of my life again.'

Another necessary stage in getting over a break-up may be a desire to return to the carefree days of adolescence and sexual experimentation – to the days before you were part of a couple, in fact. Many newly divorced people go through this phase, which is all part of the self-discovery process that inevitably follows a major life change. Having suffered the shock of being left, or leaving a marriage or long-term relationship, you may feel the need to reaffirm your identity as a sexual being who is capable of attracting a partner. This kind of slightly irresponsible, even reckless behaviour is one way of proving to yourself that you are still young and desirable. People at this stage in the break-up process aren't looking for another life partner, but for someone who will make them feel good about themselves again. They may even go through a series of these 'unsuitable' relationships, before finding someone with whom they wish to settle down.

You may feel the need to reaffirm your identity as a sexual being who is capable of attracting a partner.

'After Matt and I broke up, I went a bit mad for a while,' Jen confesses. 'I'd had years of playing the loyal, supportive wife, and where had it got me? I decided what I really needed was to have some fun. I joined a dating agency, and for a few months I was going out virtually every night – usually with a different man each time. None of these relationships lasted long, even though several of the blokes I met were actually very sweet. But it was as if I was keeping them at arm's length the whole time. Now I see that it was probably self-protection, but at the time I thought there must be something wrong with me. I'd go out with a man a couple of times, and maybe we'd go to bed together, and then I'd think, This is boring, and end it. My friends all said I was behaving like a teenager.'

Going through a phase of serial dating of this kind, adolescent as it may seem, is a harmless enough way of reasserting your sexual identity, and of getting yourself out into circulation again. Most of us enjoy the thrill of going out with someone new, and the fun of making ourselves look attractive for another person. A short-term, fairly casual relationship, in which neither partner wants long-term commitment, may be just what you need to get over the pain of a break-up – as long as you practise safe sex, and don't end up hurting anyone. Unfortunately, that is all too often the case when feelings are involved.

Rosanna, whose relationship with her boyfriend Lee ended after four years when Lee became involved with another woman, embarked on an affair with her boss as a way of 'getting her own back'. 'I was so angry with Lee, and so determined to get back at him for the way he'd treated me, that I didn't care who else I hurt in the process. Jeremy, my boss, was a lot older than me and married, with two grown-up children. I thought it would be the perfect, no-strings affair. I hadn't reckoned on falling in love.' What started as a casual affair gradually became an obsession for Rosanna. 'I did all the things you're not supposed to do: phoning him at home, badgering him about spending more time with me.

It all got a bit out of hand. Eventually, of course, his wife found out, and then all hell was let loose.'

When Jeremy ended the affair at his wife's insistence, Rosanna decided to quit her job. 'It had become impossible, working that closely with someone you're involved with. When he told me it was over, I felt it was time to get out.' Now happily living with a new boyfriend, Rosanna looks back on this phase of her life with some amazement. 'I can't believe I could have been so stupid as to think for one minute that Jeremy would give up everything else in his life for me. I suppose I was just testing the relationship to the limits. Deep down, I knew it was wrong for me. But it was a good lesson in what can happen when feelings get out of control.'

Stella, whose marriage broke up when she was in her early thirties, had a series of short-lived, fairly unsatisfactory relationships in the months that followed her divorce. 'Basically, I went wild. I was twenty-six when I got married, and thirty-one when Jon and I split. During those five years I suppose you could say I was the perfect, devoted wife – never going anywhere without Jon, and dropping a lot of my friends when we started living together. After the divorce, I can remember thinking, Right. I'm going to make up for lost time. I was determined to "show" him – and myself – that I could have more fun without him. The first affair I embarked on was with someone at work – that was a bit of a no-no from the start. He was seeing someone else at the time, so there was a lot of creeping around – I could never go to his flat, for instance, because "she" might turn up. It was exciting, I suppose, because of the danger. That broke up when Grant – my lover – decided he couldn't handle the guilt.

'Then I started going out with Darren, a much younger man, whom I'd met on a business trip. He was fun, and very good for my ego – but after a few weeks it became obvious he wasn't interested in a long-term relationship. I think I was the one to end that one! On the plane to New York for yet another business trip, I met Marco. He was my age, gorgeous, funny, intelligent and –

unfortunately – terminally unfaithful. Our affair lasted six months, and ended when I got fed up with other women leaving passionate messages on his answerphone. He swore blind they were completely innocent, but by this time it was obvious he wasn't cut out for commitment, either.

'Greg, my next boyfriend, was much more considerate – always writing me sweet letters telling me how much he missed me. The problem with him was that his job in export sales meant he was always travelling. What with my working schedule, we hardly ever saw one another! My current boyfriend, Carl, is someone I've known as a friend for a long time – in fact, he was best man at my wedding to Jon. He says he always wanted to ask me out, but thought I wasn't interested, because I always seemed to have so many men around me, and to be having such a good time. Which just goes to show how wrong you can be.'

Serial dating of the kind described in Stella's account is something most of us indulge in when we're teenagers. At age sixteen or so, the idea of settling down seems (quite rightly) a long way off, and the emphasis is on having as many partners as your GCSE revision schedule will allow. By the time most of us are ready to commit – usually in our mid- to late twenties or early thirties – being with one person for the foreseeable future suddenly doesn't seem like such a bad idea. It's then that most of us are ready to take on responsibilities, such as careers, mortgages and children. We say goodbye to the carelessness of youth and, with it, the dating game.

Or at least until we experience break-up. Suddenly, everything we took for granted – relationships, security – is turned upside down. We start behaving like the teenagers we once were, experimenting with new possibilities, reinventing ourselves to an extent. This process is partly a defiant one – we want to 'show' the world (and, most importantly, our ex-partner) that we are better off without the relationship that once sustained us. We want to prove to ourselves that we are still young and vibrant, and that we can still attract a partner. Another side of the 'second adolescence' phase most people go through after break-up is the necessary casting off of the past. It's like drawing a line under your marriage, and saying to yourself, It's over. By acting in a slightly wild and even out-of-character way, you are demonstrating that you are now a different person from the one Before Break-up. You are saying to yourself that it's time to move on.

The end of a relationship can also be a new beginning. Freed from the constraints of an unsatisfactory partnership, you can concentrate on your own needs and take steps to construct a more satisfying and fulfilling way of life. Having just got out of a relationship that *didn't* work, you can learn how to make any subsequent relationship a success, using the (hard-won) experience of the break-up. It isn't going to be easy – but, then, the most rewarding things in life seldom are. And one thing is certain: living through a divorce is one of those life-changing events that can lead to an increase, rather than a decrease, in self-confidence. It's a time in your life when – perhaps for the first time since you became an independent adult – you can take charge of your own happiness.

10
Reinventing Yourself

When a relationship ends, the emotional impact is often devastating – in fact, many counsellors treat it as a form of bereavement. You have lost not only your partner, but also the role you had as one of a couple, in addition to the extended network of family and friendships that went with it. You will have lost the daily habits and routines that were a part of the relationship, and the comforting sense of familiarity that came from them. (One friend I know couldn't face going to her local Sainsbury's for months after her divorce, because it reminded her too much of going there with her ex.) The sense of security that you derived from being with a partner, even if they turned out not to be right for you, will also have disappeared. If you are the partner who has left the family home, you may have lost contact with your children. You may have lost materially, too – having to give up your home or the standard of living you were used to.

All these and other, related, losses can undermine your confidence in yourself and your future. Getting that confidence back can be done, but, like every major life change, it takes time, and shouldn't be hurried. One of the ways of coming to terms with what has happened to you and your life is by breaking it down into stages. As with getting over the death of someone you love, getting over a broken marriage or serious relationship goes through a number of clearly defined phases. How long it takes each individual to cope with each of these of course varies a great deal. Some people adjust fairly quickly; others do not. With any break-up of a serious relationship, you can probably reckon on at least a year – and perhaps as much as two – before you are 'over' it. Understanding the various stages can be a help. Knowing that you are experiencing what a lot of other people have also experienced is comforting, too. When I told a friend I was writing this book, she said ruefully, 'I could have done with a book like that five years ago. When you're going through a divorce, you feel so isolated.'

As a society, we are now much better at talking about our emotions than we were, say, twenty years ago. A new openness about sexual and emotional experience, combined with a new kind of language for discussing problems – much of it derived from psychotherapy – has meant that we are less inhibited about such things than our parents' generation were. And yet there are still taboo areas – our attitudes towards marriage break-up being one of them. It would take a highly insensitive person to tell a newly bereaved person to 'snap out of it' and 'get on with things' – and yet that is exactly the attitude many people adopt towards the newly divorced. The sniping in the press about the twice-divorced Patsy Kensit – left on her own with two children after her husband Liam Gallagher deserted her for another woman – is a case in point, with most newspapers adopting the sneering tone that she had better find herself another 'celebrity' husband, double-quick!

Yet people (even celebrities) need time to grieve when a relationship ends. These are some of the stages you may find yourself going through during this period of emotional adjustment:

- **shock**
- **disbelief and denial**
- **sadness and depression**

- **guilt**
- **anger**
- **coming to terms with loss**

Shock is often the first reaction to the end of a relationship. It can manifest itself in various ways, but often takes the form of a kind of numbness, a refusal to believe that what is happening is really taking place. 'When Mark told me he was leaving me, I literally couldn't understand what he was saying,' recalls Caroline. 'It was as if he'd started talking in a foreign language. I can remember thinking, I'm being very calm about this, but the truth was I didn't know how to react, because it all seemed so unreal. It was only much later, after Mark had actually left the house, that I was able to cry.'

When you are in shock, you can't think straight, and you may find yourself acting oddly or out of character – losing the car keys, or forgetting to pick up the children from school. You may be prone to panic attacks, loss of appetite or sudden exhaustion. All these are symptoms of shock – which is your body's defence mechanism against unbearable feelings. Only when you are ready to grapple with painful emotions (which could take a few days, or even weeks) will you be ready to move on to the next stage.

Disbelief and denial are very common reactions to the news that a relationship has ended. If you have been left by your partner, it can be very hard to accept that he or she will not come back eventually. Although most people come to terms with the truth within a few weeks or perhaps months, it can take longer than that if one or other partner refuses to 'let go'. Sometimes this happens when a couple continue to have a sexual relationship, even after the marriage has broken down and they are no longer living together. One friend continued to have sex with her ex-partner for almost a year after they split, in the hope that he would realise what he was missing and come back to her. Eventually she sought counselling, and was able to end the relationship, and to accept that her marriage was over.

Sadness and depression may occur throughout the grieving process. They affect both partners, but may be more acute in the one who has been left. 'After Stevie went, I was a complete basket case for months,' says Paolo. 'I couldn't stand to listen to any of the music we'd listened to together, or watch any of the television programmes we'd liked, because they reminded me of her. I stopped eating and just lay about the flat for days at a time, staring at the wall. Even going out was a nightmare, because I was bound to run into someone who knew us as a couple. I turned into a bit of a recluse during that time.' Even though sadness is a painful emotion, it is healthy to experience it when you have suffered the 'bereavement' of divorce and separation. By giving in to your feelings – crying at a familiar song, or feeling pangs of regret at a particular memory – you are allowing the healing process to work. Stifling such feelings, by pretending that everything is OK, can only delay getting them out of your system.

Guilt is an inevitable part of breaking up, whether you are the person who has initiated the separation or not. If you are the person who has left the relationship, you may feel guilt towards your former partner, and towards any children of the relationship. If you are the one who has been left, you may feel guilty about having 'failed' in your marriage. 'I felt dreadful for months after I left Rachel,' recalls Tim. 'Partly it was because it was my fault the marriage ended the way it did, and partly it was because I felt guilty about leaving the children. It was a really horrible feeling, knowing that Rachel blamed me for what happened, and that the kids might grow up hating me. That was one of the reasons I wanted to try counselling – so as to deal with the guilt about it all.'

Anger channels negative emotions, which, turned inward, can take the form of depression. It is a commonplace of therapy to talk about 'getting in touch with your anger' – and, up to a point, this is a healthy thing to do. Feeling angry with your partner for ending the relationship is perfectly natural, and – if it's kept within reasonable limits (not involving violent behaviour) – expressing that anger can be an essential stage in getting over break-up. Writing an angry letter telling your ex precisely what you think of them is one example of using anger constructively. Joining a gym and working off some of your feelings of rage on the treadmill or exercise bike is another. Anger is one of those emotions that are better out than in, so screaming loudly in the middle of a wide, open space or smashing that vase you always hated is likely to make you feel instantly better. Bottling up your anger for years and years – or, worse, acting it out in extreme or violent ways – is not.

'When John and I decided to part, I was terribly calm about it all for ages,' recalls Louise. 'A lot of my friends commented on how "well" I was taking it, and I didn't find it difficult picking up the threads of my life at all – carrying on with work, and doing all the things I'd always done. Then, one day, about six months after we split, I was clearing out a cupboard and I came across the dinner service we'd been given by John's parents as a wedding present. I know it was very expensive, but I'd never liked it – it was far too ornate – so I'd just put it away and only used it on the rare occasions my in-laws came round. When I saw it, my first thought was to send it to the local charity shop. But, as I was packing it up, one of the plates slipped out of my hand and smashed on the floor. I didn't even stop to think. A few minutes later, every single plate and dish in the set was broken. I'd thrown them all at the wall, screaming at the top of my lungs. By the end, I was sobbing and crying. I'm sure it did me the world of good, to let out all that anger. Afterwards I swept up all the broken china, made myself a cup of tea – and sent a donation to the charity I'd intended to give the dinner service to. I've never told anybody about it until now.'

Coming to terms with loss is what happens when you have accepted that your relationship is over and you are ready to move on. People who have come through this process often describe a new and satisfying feeling of 'wholeness'. They no longer feel that part of them is 'missing' – nor that they are incomplete without their former partner. They feel ready to stand on their own two feet and cope with what the world has to offer. As feelings of depression, guilt and anger fall away, they find that life suddenly seems to have more to offer, as positive emotions come to the fore. They may even feel a sense of pride and achievement in having coped with the divorce as well as they have done. Even though it may take months or even years before you reach this stage, you know you have reached it when you no longer feel resentful about the past, and when you can forgive your ex – and yourself – for what went wrong in your relationship. You can work towards recovery. It isn't something that happens overnight – but it does happen.

At this stage, it can sometimes help to take a good, hard look at yourself, and every aspect of your life and aspirations. Are you the sort of person you want to be? Are you leading the sort of life you want? If not, why not?

What's holding you back?

Low self-esteem often has its roots in childhood, and the end of a relationship can also be experienced as a failure. Something so central to your life, in which you invested your hopes and your commitment, has gone wrong. No wonder you doubt whether you have what it takes to determine the course of your life in the future, or to find lasting happiness.

Developing confidence is not easy, but it can be done. First, you have to know yourself. Think about the kind of person you are, and the side of yourself you show to other people. It can help to make a rough chart, setting out these various aspects of yourself. Try to be as honest as possible (no one else needs to see this). You may find some of it surprising!

- **Describe the person you show to the world** – the person your colleagues know at work, for example. Is he/she confident, assertive, well-groomed, positive in outlook? Or shy, retiring, lacking in confidence, self-effacing? How much responsibility does this person have, in his/her daily life? Is this person generally competent – or does he/she have difficulty in completing tasks? Does this person give an impression of happiness or unhappiness? (You'll know this from others' comments – 'Cheer up, it may never happen!' is often a clumsy but well-intentioned way of saying, 'I'm worried about you. You look so unhappy.')
- **Describe the person you feel you are inside.** If you're the confident/assertive type at work, are you as confident when you're by yourself, or is there another side to you? Do you feel insecure at times, and feel that no one likes you? Conversely, if you feel you come across as shy and insecure to other people, is this how you feel all the time? Or is there another self – bolder and more confident – you conceal from others, because you're afraid how they might react, if they knew the 'real' you?
- **Describe the person you'd like to be** (and no, I *don't* mean one who looks like Michelle Pfeiffer!). Everyone has hidden potential and aspirations they don't mention to others, because they fear ridicule. As children, we can all remember playing the 'When I grow up I want to be...' game. So play it now. What do you want to be when you 'grow up'? Are there dreams and desires you haven't yet fulfilled? Would you like to be a more confident, cheerful, easygoing person – or do you

feel you need to be more assertive/forceful/determined? All these characteristics are a part of everyone, in varying degrees. How they affect your behaviour – and your future – depends entirely on you.

Learning how to enjoy life again

So what can you do to make yourself feel in charge of your life again? And is there any tried and tested formula for restoring self-confidence and that indefinable something the French call *joie de vivre*? Certainly physical fitness is a vital part of the recovery process. Not only is it of obvious benefit to one's general health, but recent studies have shown that there is a definite link between physical and psychological wellbeing. Simply, when you exercise, you raise your levels of serotonin – the chemical in the brain that controls mood and counteracts depression. Serotonin levels also drop when there is a deficiency of light, giving rise to seasonal affective disorder (SAD), which affects people during the darker winter months, and explains why most of us feel better on a warm, sunny day. So exercising – whether this means joining a gym, going to aerobics classes or deciding to cycle to work rather than take the car – is very high on the list of 'things to do', when you're getting over a divorce.

With far greater health awareness, and the increase in fitness facilities across the country, it is now easier than ever to find a class or gym that suits you, and that can be fitted in as part of your daily or weekly routine. Obviously, this will vary, depending on individual needs and wants. You may find you prefer to join one of the growing number of rambling clubs springing up around the country, or to get into the habit of going for a lunchtime swim, rather than to get stuck into the more punishing routines of weightlifting and circuit training (although even these are less intimidating than they sound). The point is, getting your body back in shape is a fast-track way of feeling – and looking – good. It's all about learning to like yourself again. About reminding yourself that you're an attractive, vital person – someone who enjoys life, and intends to get the most out of it.

Getting fit can help you

- get in touch with your physical self
- improve general health and sleeping patterns
- banish depression
- improve your skin, hair and figure
- feel younger and more vital
- meet new people

Getting fit is not primarily about fitting yourself back into that size 10 dress, or those 28-waist jeans – although weight loss and improved muscle tone can be a pleasant side effect! Most people who exercise regularly find that it has positive effects on both physical appearance and overall confidence. If you look good, you feel happier and more attractive – it's as simple as that. For anyone who has been through a break-up, it can take time to rebuild the confidence you have lost. Going to the gym is a great start, but it's far from being the only route to regaining that inner glow. It may sound trite, but being nice to yourself is also an important part of the recovery process. If you've been through a hard time, you deserve a break – maybe a few self-indulgent treats wouldn't go amiss, either.

One of the clichés about newly divorced people (particularly if they are women) is the idea that all it takes is a 'makeover' – a new hairstyle, a facial, a new wardrobe or a bit of minor corrective surgery – to make them feel good about themselves again. Can it really be as simple as all that to turn your life around? Well, yes and no. While it would be foolish to suggest that a trip to the hairdresser's (say) will mend a broken heart, or that buying yourself a new outfit is going to revolutionise your social life, it has to be said that neither will do you any harm. If you've come through the trauma of break-up, with all the misery and self-doubt such an experience entails, you probably need a bit of TLC – and, if no one else is there to give it to you, then you have to get it for yourself. Getting yourself a really good haircut or treating yourself to a fabulous frock may not make your problems disappear – but it's certainly a pleasant distraction from them.

Similarly, treating yourself to a bunch of fresh flowers, or a really nice bottle of wine to go with the cauliflower cheese you were planning for supper, or splashing out on a manicure, or a CD of your favourite opera, or a night out with a friend to see the new George Clooney film may all sound self-indulgent. But, believe me, they're not. You deserve some fun. Life's too short not to enjoy yourself. And when you're getting over a break-up you sometimes need reminding just how much fun life can be. Because – hold onto the thought – life is going to get better from now on. You've been through the hard part – the heartache and shock, and the feelings of rage and resentment – and you've come out the other side. Now you've got the chance to make a fresh start. Of course, there is no set formula for doing this. But you could start by making yourself feel good about life again – and that means being nice to yourself.

- Book that holiday you've been dreaming about –you deserve it
- Treat yourself to a facial and sauna – because you're worth it
- Invest in a really good pair of shoes
- Leave the kids with their grandmother (she offered) and go shopping
- Get theatre or cinema tickets
- Buy yourself an extravagant bunch of flowers
- Cook a meal using all your favourite ingredients
- Get a very good haircut
- Ring that old friend you've been meaning to contact – go on, just *do* it

- Go for a brisk country walk followed by a pub lunch
- Revisit your favourite painting in your local art gallery
- Play your favourite CD at top volume (when the neighbours are out)
- Buy yourself a stack of new novels and read them

Everyone is different, and each person will have their own ways of coping with the day-to-day realities of being single again. For some, the process of self-discovery may involve a complete change of lifestyle. One friend 'celebrated' her divorce by moving to New York, changing her job, her friends and her wardrobe in one fell swoop! Others may prefer a more gradualist approach – learning a language, or going to life-drawing classes, or taking up a sport they haven't tried before. The benefits of this are twofold: first and most importantly, you're doing something for *you* – because you want to do it – and, secondly, you might get to meet some new people in the process.

If you were married young and spent your twenties and early thirties raising children, you may not have had the time or inclination to explore your creative potential fully. Similarly, the demands of combining a career with marriage can often be all-absorbing. As a newly single person, you find yourself at a crossroads in your life. Marriage and having children may be behind you, but a lot of other possibilities lie ahead. So, as well as getting your body back in shape, it's worth giving your mind and spirit a look-in as well! Most alternative health centres run classes in meditation and relaxation, and there are weekend 'retreats' you can sign up for as well, which offer the spiritual equivalent of a detox fast at a health farm. Or, if such 'New Age' activities don't appeal, then how about getting yourself on the mailing list for your local theatre or concert hall, and expanding your cultural horizons a bit? Or signing up for those salsa classes you always said you never had time for? You owe it to yourself to make the most of your new life.

So, even though the advice often dispensed by agony aunts and well-meaning friends about 'joining an evening class' as the best way to meet new people sounds like a cliché, it does contain a grain of common sense. If you're doing something you enjoy for its own sake, you're going to feel happier all round. And happy people are more attractive and fun to be with. It doesn't necessarily mean you'll meet Mr (or Ms) Right the very first time you walk into your local adult education centre to sign on for beginner's Spanish, or that the person of your dreams will be sitting in the next seat at that special showing of *Brief Encounter* – but there's always a possibility.

'Joining an evening class' is traditionally one of the best ways to meet new people – although it should be borne in mind that not all of them will be ideal romantic partners.

And, even if you don't meet anyone, you're still going to gain from the experience, because, for someone else to like you, you first have to like yourself. You have to be the sort of person – interesting, informed, well balanced and attractive – *you'd* cross the street to meet. Going through divorce damages your self-esteem; this is all about getting it back. It has to be said, too, that a lot of people who've been going through a divorce feel too emotionally bruised by the experience to want to cope straight away with the demands of a new relationship. So go easy on yourself. Don't think that, just because you aren't rushing out to parties every night, and making the most of your new-found freedom, there must be something the matter with you. The healing process takes time. Sometimes it's the little things – like going shopping with a friend after work or having an evening in with a good book – that help you through this period the most. Learning to enjoy your own company is a major step on the way to full recovery from the trauma of break-up.

Things you can do for a 'fresh-start' feeling

- Redecorate your flat/house – or move house, if that s an option
- Start applying for new jobs – or ask for that pay rise
- Learn a language – you'll need it, for next year's adventure holiday
- Learn to dance – waltz, salsa, tango, jive . . . just get moving
- Learn to cook – you can do better than macaroni cheese
- Join a yoga class – isn't it time you learned how to relax?
- Learn to paint, write, play an instrument – unleash those creative powers
- Learn to ski – next Christmas could find you on the piste
- Learn to ride – haven't you always fancied yourself as Lorna Doone?
- Throw a party – invite all your friends and celebrate being single!

A major life change such as divorce shakes you up and rearranges everything you thought was fixed and settled. It forces you to take a long hard look at yourself, and the kind of life you've been leading up to now. Are you happy with the way things are – or are there areas of your life that could be improved? Getting

over a major life change such as a divorce can be a liberating as
well as an unsettling experience, involving a kind of emotional
stocktaking. It sometimes helps at this stage to make a list of all
the things you like about yourself (and your life) and all the things
you'd like to change. Because what you're going through at the
moment is all about developing your potential – not stifling it. It's
all about expanding your capacity for enjoyment.

- Make a list of twenty things you like about yourself – for
  example, 'I'm resourceful, intelligent, considerate, fun to be
  with and attractive; I'm a good mother, a loyal friend, a reliable
  worker and a responsible citizen; I'm good at making things
  with my hands, and I've got a good eye for design; I'm a good
  cook, and my dinner parties are always a hit with my friends;
  people turn to me in trouble, because I'm a sympathetic
  listener; I'm able to admit my mistakes, and try to learn from
  them; I'm unselfish, and always try to put others' needs before
  my own; I can laugh at myself, and I seldom complain about
  my problems to my friends; I'm generous, thoughtful and
  generally good-tempered.'
- Make a list of twenty things you d like to change about
  yourself – for example, 'I'm stubborn, and always think I
  know best about everything; I have a tendency to be a bit of a
  martyr; I worry too much; I sometimes have trouble sleeping;
  I don't like asking for help; I find it difficult to relax; I can be
  judgmental; I'm occasionally sharp with the children; I find it
  hard to forgive; I get upset when trivial things go wrong; I have
  a tendency to panic when I'm in a hurry; I can be overcritical;
  I hate being late; I can't stand untidiness; I'm a bit of a "control
  freak"; I'm sometimes forgetful; I have a tendency to
  depression; I overeat when I'm unhappy; I have a tendency to
  blame others when things go wrong.'
- Compare the two lists and see if they overlap in any way – for
  instance, the same independence of mind that makes a person

'resourceful' can, if taken too far, turn into stubbornness. The perfectionism that makes your dinner parties such a success may also be the thing that makes you overcritical and sharp. Maybe you need to lighten up a little, stop worrying so much about what people think of you, leave the dishes until morning. Most of us are aware that we have faults but don't know how to go about changing them. Sometimes all it takes is a determined effort! One friend who drew up a like/dislike list was struck by the fact that she'd listed all the things her friends said they liked about her, rather than try to come up with her own list. She was what is known as a 'people-pleaser' – anxious about the effect she had on others, and scared of saying anything that might make other people dislike her. She decided to sign up for an assertiveness-training course, which helped her get over her fear of being disliked. She found a new confidence, which spilled over into her career and even her love life! Sometimes, making a fresh start is just about taking a long, hard look at the life you've got, and deciding what you value about it.

Thinking positively about your life is one way of coping with the day-to-day stresses of being newly single. It's not a new idea by any means – your grandmother probably called it 'counting your blessings'. You can apply the method described about to your life in general. Make a list of ten (or twenty) things you like about your life. These can be big things, such as the fact that you're in good health, or that you've got lots of friends, or that you enjoy your job; or little things, such as the fact that your bedroom gets the sun in the mornings, or you've got the new Joanna Trollope novel to read, or that three people told you today that they liked your new haircut. Then write down ten (or twenty) things you'd like to change. Again, these can be big or small. You've always hated the colour of this room. You wish you were half a stone lighter. You wish you were better at saying no to people. Obviously, not all of these will be things you can change as easily as, say, stopping off at the DIY store to buy a couple of cans of emulsion with which to transform an unattractive room, but it's worth thinking about the areas of your life that could improve, given time and effort.

Ten things I like about my life
- I have lots of friends
- I have a supportive family
- I have a lot of interests
- I get to travel a lot
- I live in a nice house
- I'm fit and healthy
- I'm never bored
- I can enjoy the good things in life
- I finally got round to reading *War and Peace*
- I've got a nice bottle of Chablis in the fridge

Ten things I'd like to change about my life
- I'd like more time to pursue my own interests
- I'd like not to have to worry so much about money
- I'd like not to have to worry so much
- I'd like to be able to spend some time in another country
- I'd like to be more creative
- I'd like to spend more time with my children
- I'd like to have a more flexible work schedule
- I'd like to learn a language
- I'd like to be fitter
- I'd like to get rid of the horrible carpet in the sitting room

When you have your list, take a look at it, then put it away somewhere safe. You don't need it any more. In a year's time, take another look at it and see how many of the 'things to change' you've changed. All of them? You *have* been working hard on yourself. None of them? Maybe, after all, your life was pretty good the way it was. Some of them? You're on the road to your new life, because having the *will* to change your life is half the battle – even if you can't do it all overnight.

11
Being Single Can Be Fun

So you're fit, healthy and happy. You look great and all your friends tell you that it's time you met someone new. A year ago you'd have laughed at the very idea. Why on earth would I want to get involved with anyone else? you probably asked. I've got plenty of friends, thank you very much. I don't *need* anyone else in my life. But now you're not so sure they haven't got a point. Maybe you should get out with members of the opposite sex more. You deserve a bit of fun, after all. Yes, on balance, you'd like to meet someone new. The question is, where are you going to meet them? You're not a teenager any more; you can't go to the sort of clubs you frequented when you were eighteen. Most of your friends are boring old marrieds, who seem to know only other boring old marrieds. You can't face the thought of *advertising* – can you?

'I was very prejudiced against the whole idea of meeting a man through an ad,' admits Janine, a divorcee now in her late thirties, who runs a small West End gallery. 'I had friends who'd met their partners that way, of course – but I always thought it wasn't for me. There seemed to be something so embarrassing about the whole process – choosing a lover the way you'd choose a second-hand car. It just wasn't my style. But then I was working such long hours at the gallery, hanging shows and dealing with clients, that I just wasn't getting to meet anyone new. Even when there were parties and private views, I was generally the hostess, making sure everyone *else* was having a good time. I certainly didn't have time to talk to any of the people who came to the shows, however much I might have wanted to!'

A friend persuaded her to join a dating agency aimed at single, professional people. 'I gave it a try for a year. They match your details up on computer with those of men in roughly the same age and income bracket, and then sift out the ones who don't fit the physical profile you've specified. It was all very professionally done, and I did meet several quite presentable men, one of whom I went out with for a few months. But in the end the relationship petered out, mainly because Paul wasn't ready to give up his bachelor lifestyle and commit to a serious relationship. I've since learned that quite a lot of men use dating agencies this way – in order to maintain a constant supply of willing females. You just have to watch out for the type, I suppose.'

After the setback with Paul, Janine was reluctant to go through the same process again, until a friend persuaded her to place her own ad in the *Guardian* 'Soulmates' column. 'Liz said it was much easier this way, because it was anonymous. You place your ad, and then people ring a message line and leave a voicemail message with their telephone number. The ones you like the sound of, you then arrange to meet – always in a public place, of course – without divulging any details about yourself until you're sure you want to. I had about fifty people replying to my ad. I arranged to meet eight of them. Andrew was the seventh. I remember thinking, Well, I can cancel that one tomorrow night, now... He told me afterwards he fell in love with me the minute he set eyes on me. I have to say, it's restored my faith in romantic love.'

Zoe, a primary school teacher with two children now in their teens, was no less reluctant about finding a partner through the small ads. 'After my divorce nine years ago, I immersed myself in the children and work, in that order. The idea of starting a new relationship didn't even figure. Since all the male staff at the school where I work are either married or a lot younger than I am, there was never any chance of meeting someone that way. Most of my friends are married or in long-term relationships. Those that aren't are all women! So it was next to impossible to find anyone new by the conventional channels. I did go on a couple of adventure holidays by myself when the kids were a bit older, but, even though I enjoyed these very much, I didn't end up meeting the man of my dreams.

'Then Sharon, a close friend, suggested I should try the ads, because another friend of ours – also a divorcee – had met her new partner that way. I thought she was joking at first, but agreed to give it a try. The first few I rang sounded nice on the whole, but there were things I found offputting. For instance, some men specified they wanted someone much younger (I'm forty-two), so even those that gave their age as in their forties wanted to meet a woman of twenty-five! Then there were the ones that said they were "very good-looking". I've been told I'm fairly good-looking myself, but I tend to think you should let other people decide about things like that!

'In the end, I decided to put my own ad in, because Sharon said I was much too fussy and it was the only way I'd ever find what I was looking for! I was staggered at the response. The first week, I had about thirty replies, and about the same in the second week. It was very flattering, even though it was obvious that I couldn't meet all the men who'd called me. I selected a short list of about twelve. We arranged to meet at the National Gallery and places like that – because it's always easier to make your excuses and leave, if you don't like the look of someone when you're in a public place, than if you're trapped in some restaurant. The first guy I met was nice but not really my type. It's a shame, because you keep wanting to reassure someone that they're bound to find somebody nice soon – even though it's not going to be you!

'It was the same with the second and third. All the men I met asked to see me again, which was very good for my ego! But I knew it would be unfair to agree to another meeting if there was no chance of the relationship developing into something more serious. Then I met Alan. From the very first moment, I just knew I wanted to see him again. All through the date, I kept hoping he felt the same. We went for a meal and I kept thinking, God, he's lovely. I can't believe he's single. I didn't want to seem too eager, so I left it a couple of days before I rang him. He's told me since that he was going out of his mind during those two days, wondering whether he'd hear from me again. We've been together a year now, and it just gets better and better.'

Fairytale happy endings apart, getting started on the dating game after years of being out of it can be an intimidating prospect. The chances are that, if you've been in a long relationship, the majority of your friends will be couples, whose circle of friends, in turn, will also mainly consist of other couples. Even if your work brings you into contact with other unattached people, it is often difficult (and not always advisable) to effect the transition from work colleague to friend. You aren't the sort of person who chats easily to people you don't know, at the gym or in your local wine bar. So just how do you go about meeting someone new?

Dinner parties

Every single woman dreads the moment when, after greeting her at the door, the hostess murmurs, 'Do come and meet so-and-so. He's single, too . . . ' and she knows she's about to be Set Up once again. Over the past few years, well-meaning friends have tried this tactic on me on numerous occasions, with varying degrees of success. There was the time when, just after taking my coat, the friend who'd invited me to dinner 'just to meet a few people, because you probably don't get out much these days' whispered, 'I hope you and [X] get on. He's ever so sweet, but I've never

Single women dread the moment when their hostess murmurs,
'Meet "X". He's single too...'

been able to work out whether or not he's gay.' Another time, I was seated next to a man who seemed initially like a dream date – tall, blond, good-looking and (by his own account) rich. His conversation, however, consisted entirely of talking about his car (a Porsche, naturally) and the number of times he'd sent food back in restaurants. A third dinner-party date from hell was the man who was just going through his second divorce, and spent the entire meal ranting about his ex-wife. 'I thought you two would have something in common,' said my hostess, when I berated her for inflicting him on me.

Horror stories apart, dinner parties are often good places to meet new people in an informal setting. The advantages are that you'll probably know at least some of the other people there, so you'll be relaxed and appear at your best. The addition of good food and wine adds to the convivial atmosphere, and makes this one of the most stress-free ways of getting to know someone. Even if he's too shy to ask you for your number at the end of the evening, there's always the chance that – having checked with your hostess that you're currently unattached – he might call you afterwards. One friend of mine actually went so far as to slip her business card into the breast pocket of a man she'd met and liked at a dinner party. 'It let him know I wanted to see him again, without being too forward,' she says. 'I was just praying he wouldn't send that jacket to the cleaner's, before he retrieved the card...' Fortunately, he didn't, and he did call her. The last I heard, they were giving dinner parties together.

Singles bars

A relatively new idea in Britain, the singles bar was imported here from the States, where the concept has been established for years. Basically, there are two kinds of singles bar. The first, generally aimed at a slightly older age group (early thirties upwards), caters exclusively to a single clientele, and offers, as well as the bar itself, additional attractions in the form of a variety of areas for dancing and 'sitting out', where single people can meet and get to know each other. The second, while not aimed solely at single people, tends to cater mainly to a younger, predominantly single crowd – updating the traditional idea of pubs and social clubs as primarily for men into something both sexes can share. It is this variety that has become the more successful in Britain, which already has a long tradition of bars as meeting places (i.e. pubs), so that wine bar chains such as All Bar One, whose décor and ambience is aimed as much at women as men, have become part of the urban landscape.

The good thing about these establishments, as opposed to most pubs, is that it is perfectly acceptable for a woman on her own to have a drink there, without feeling that she will have to put up with unwanted attention. Most single women develop an antenna, which makes them aware of potentially embarrassing or threatening situations, and I have to say that, in several years of meeting friends in the new 'women-friendly' bars, I have never felt at a disadvantage because of my gender. I also have to say that I've never met a man under these circumstances (maybe because most of them are *too* polite and well behaved!), although I do have friends who have. And, certainly, they are pleasant places to spend an evening in relaxed surroundings – which is sometimes all one feels like doing, after all.

Purpose-designed singles bars (such as Tiger, Tiger in Whitehall) are a different kettle of fish altogether. Then, it helps if you are young, 'fit' and 'up for it' – even though many of the people who go there in search of a partner are none of these things. My friend Debbie, who is divorced, went there just after she'd celebrated her fortieth birthday. 'I thought I'd be the oldest person there, but actually there were quite a lot of people in their late thirties and older,' she recalls. 'There are several floors, so you can choose the kind of music you'd like to hear – loud and raunchy, or softer, easy-listening stuff. I like dancing, so I chose the disco bit. There were loads of blokes just standing about, so I grabbed one and said, "Do you fancy a bop?" Lynne, the friend I went with, thought I'd gone mad, but that's the whole point of a place like that. There's no sense in being a shrinking violet.'

Bookshops

If the idea of braving a singles bar is too much for you, then try a visit to your local bookshop – especially if this happens to be one of the 'new-look' branches of chains such as Borders, Ottakars, Dillons or Waterstones, which have adopted the customer-friendly approach of their American and European cousins. Because here you'll find a lot more than just books (although you will still find those, thankfully). As well as the latest novels, biographies or cookery books, you'll find CDs, magazines, greetings cards and – most importantly – a café. It's here that, surrounded by the pleasant aroma of cappuccino and café latte, and with the latest newspapers, glossies and contemporary fiction to peruse at your table, you'll find yourself in the company of like-minded – and hopefully unattached – bibliophiles.

It's a more subtle form of singles bar, if you like, and one with a uniquely relaxed atmosphere. Talking to someone across a table in a room full of people about a subject that interests you both ('Is that the new Julian Barnes? I've just read that. What did you think?') is a lot easier than trying to get to know someone in a noisy, crowded bar. There's a similar atmosphere in these 'bookshop/cafés' to that of the *cafés philosophiques* you find everywhere in France – places where you can sit and read, or chat, without feeling under any kind of pressure. One friend met the man she is now happily involved with when both found themselves going for the last seat at a reading held at one of the big London bookstores. He (gallantly) let her have the chair, while he sat down on the floor. At the interval, being a liberated type, she insisted that they swap. What really clinched it was when he bought a copy of the book they'd heard being read – and got the author to dedicate it 'To Elizabeth' (which is my friend's name). A true meeting of minds, one might think.

Evening classes

Joining an evening class is traditionally one of the best ways to meet new people – although it should be borne in mind that not all of them will be ideal romantic partners. Since a high proportion of those attending adult education classes are retired people, women with young children, or A-level students putting in a bit of extra study, it stands to reason that eligible types are few and far between. In the ten years or so that I've been going to classes in subjects ranging from French conversation ('Ooh, la la!') to life drawing, I can honestly say that, although I've met a lot of lovely people of both sexes, I haven't come across anyone I'd want as a life partner. However (and there's always a 'however'), I do know others who've been luckier, falling into conversation (and ultimately into bed) with the gorgeous chap in the do-it-yourself car maintenance class, or the shy ingénue at the drama workshop. One friend had a torrid – though sadly short-lived – affair with her advanced-ceramics tutor. Another was in the queue signing up for beginners' Spanish, when she spotted a man she fancied putting his name down for Greek and Roman history. She switched queues, got his telephone number under the pretext of wanting to borrow some essential book, and now they're planning an island-hopping tour of ancient Classical sites. Serendipity, or what?

Dating agencies

A glance at the back pages of *Time Out*, the *Guardian Guide* or *Cosmopolitan* – or indeed any of the small-ads sections of any national newspaper or magazine – will reveal a bewildering choice of ads aimed at single people, ranging from those for Internet chat lines to those for dining clubs and 'introduction services' (a.k.a. dating agencies). Of these, the most reputable will generally charge a fee, which can be from £500 upwards and is nonrefundable. For this, you will receive the details from at least six other people whose background information has been matched with yours. In some cases, you will be offered the chance to meet in informal circumstances – such as at a restaurant – with other single people of both sexes, before deciding if you wish to pursue a particular relationship. Other agencies will match your details on computer with those of prospective suitors, and will then provide you with photographs or a video of a number of suitable candidates, from whom you can then select (details in all cases are confidential). Some agencies (Drawing Down the Moon, for instance) make a feature of having only 'professional people' on their books (e.g. doctors, lawyers, teachers, academics and media types). Others are more eclectic, preferring to focus on compatibility through shared interests and hobbies, rather than income bracket.

As with anything, dating agencies have their aficionados and their detractors. I know at least two friends, both busy professional types, who met their spouses this way. In Sally's case, joining a dating agency was not something she'd seriously considered until she was in her early forties. 'I'd been divorced for five years, and been out with a few people in that time, but there was never anyone special,' she recalls. 'When I joined OnlySingles, it seemed like a bit of a joke. I went out with a couple of guys, who were nice but not for me, and I was just starting to think it had been a waste of time and money when I met Daniel. That was it for me. The minute I saw him I thought,

At last ... He says it was the same for him.'

Sam, an overworked GP whose first marriage also ended in divorce, was equally cynical about the idea of finding a partner through an agency. 'I told myself I'd give it a go, because it would be a nice change to meet some women who weren't either fellow doctors, or otherwise connected with the medical profession. I never thought anything serious would come of it.' Again, his first few dates were somewhat less than ideal. 'There was one woman who talked all the time about how awful all the men she'd been out with previously had been, and how badly they'd treated her. It wasn't exactly what you'd call a fun evening ... '

Then he met Jenny. 'I liked the way she looked in her photograph, straight off. Also I liked the fact that she worked in the arts, so I knew we wouldn't end up talking shop like some of the medics I'd been out with! On the way to the date (they'd arranged to meet in the coffee shop at the National Theatre) I felt quite nervous. I kept wondering what she'd be like, and hoping she'd be as lovely as her photograph. Within seconds I knew she was the one.'

The thing that puts many people off joining a dating agency – apart from embarrassment – is of course the cost. This can vary greatly, but in general it certainly isn't cheap. Even for high-income professionals, finding the £500 to £1,500 it costs to join one of the more exclusive introduction services is justifiable only if it brings results. However 'scientific' their methods of matching people, dating agencies can provide only the raw material for romance. The spark that turns an encounter between two people into something more explosive can come only from the people themselves.

Lonely hearts

Every week in the back pages of national newspapers and magazines, fit, outgoing Ms with GSOH seek slim, sophist, attract Fs for f/ship and much more, indpdt, fun-loving Fs WLTM sim Ms with interests in film and travel, and romantic Ms hope for shy, sensitive (and pref blonde) Fs to spoil... Yes, it's the world of the lonely-hearts columns, with their enticing glimpses of alternative futures, shared with the significant other of your dreams. Just think – a year from now you could be sharing 'fun, frolics and fireside cuddles' with a nature-loving type from Yorkshire, or enjoying 'good food, wine and conversation' with a theatre fanatic from Surrey. You could be jetting off to Paris with that caring, creative professional (north London), or living it up in New York with that tactile, Sagittarian nonsmoker.

The main drawback of meeting a partner through the small ads, rather than through an agency, is that you have to carry out the screening process yourself. You don't get to see a photograph of the person you want to contact (unless you're doing this online) and the most you'll have to go on is the way his or her voice sounds on the telephone, and the – usually fairly guarded – information people leave in a voice message. That said, it's surprising how much you can glean even from this. The way a person's voice sounds and the things they say can tell you an awful lot about the kind of person they are – even if you've never set eyes on them.

'It was definitely Tom's voice I fell in love with,' says Claire, who met her current boyfriend, a teacher, through the *Guardian* 'Soulmates' columns. 'It sounded so lovely and deep. The things he'd said in his voice message were thoughtful and quite witty, too. It made me feel I'd like to meet him.' Claire, a divorcee in her thirties with two small children, had initially been nervous of the idea of advertising. 'I'd looked at some of the ads, and even rung a couple of the numbers to listen to what people said about themselves, but I never thought I'd end up placing an ad myself. I dithered about it for months, until a friend persuaded me to go ahead. In fact, it wasn't as terrifying as I'd thought. The worst part was the actual meeting, because you never know whether someone's going to measure up to the image you've got of them in your head. There's this awful split second when you first see each other, and you're both thinking the same thing – Is this the one? It can come as a shock, if you're expecting Mr Darcy and he looks more like Homer Simpson! But when I met Tom he was every bit as gorgeous as his voice.'

If, like Claire, you decide to take the advertising route to finding a new partner, it's worth bearing certain basic rules in mind. Never *ever* divulge your telephone number or address until you feel one hundred per cent certain that the person you're dealing with is trustworthy. Trust your instincts. If you don't like the way a conversation is going, hang up. Or – if you have to be polite – say, 'I'll call you back...' (having of course taken the precaution of dialling 141 before you made the call in the first place). Arrange to meet your 'date' in a public place (coffee shops, wine bars, art galleries and railway stations are all good) and *always* tell someone where you are going, and whom you are going to meet. One friend who was a bit uncertain about the man she'd arranged to meet asked a girlfriend to ring her on her mobile after an hour, to check that things were going OK and to give her an excuse to leave if she needed it. When the phone went, she was enjoying herself so much that she just hissed, 'Everything's fine. I'll call you later' – much to the amusement of her date.

Such precautions may seem extreme – but it's always better to be safe than sorry. Marianne, who allowed herself to be pressured into giving her phone number to a man she met through the small ads in a national newspaper, ended up having to change her telephone number and go ex-directory in order to avoid being pestered by him. 'Looking back, I realise I did all the wrong things,' she recalls. 'From the very first time I spoke to Philip on the phone I knew there was something not quite right going on. He was incredibly charming and smooth, and kept saying really nice things about me – like what a sexy voice I had, and how intelligent I sounded in my ad – but it was all a bit much, somehow. I nearly didn't turn up to the meeting – but then I thought how awful he'd feel, waiting and waiting, so in the end I went.

'We'd arranged to meet at an expensive restaurant, which he'd insisted on taking me to – even though I'd suggested just meeting for a coffee somewhere. When I got there, I realised at once that I didn't want a relationship with him. It wasn't that he was unattractive, or anything – just very overbearing and persistent. He kept commenting on my appearance – asking me why I didn't get my hair cut a certain way, and saying what a great figure I had. All during the meal, he kept staring at me, unnervingly, and saying that he felt we'd been "destined" to meet.

'When the bill came, he insisted on paying, and then started talking about how he'd love to take me to Paris for the weekend. I suppose I was just overwhelmed by it all – so much so that I stupidly gave him my number as I was leaving the restaurant. As soon as I walked in the door, the phone started ringing. He said he'd got tickets for some play or other, and did I want to go? When I fobbed him off, he acted very offended, saying that he thought we'd "agreed" to meet, and why was I backing out now? For the next few weeks, he pestered me with calls – sometimes acting as if nothing had happened, sometimes being quite nasty – asking me to go out with him, and saying that he was "determined" to win me round. When I told him I'd met someone else, he got quite abusive – but later rang me back to apologise, begging me to give him "one more chance".

'In the end, I had to call BT's Nuisance Call helpline for advice. They said to monitor the frequency of the calls, and keep a record of any that were particularly unpleasant, and then either tell the police or make an application to have my number changed – which is what I did, eventually. But it made me realise how careful you have to be, giving out personal information.'

The thought of having to go through an experience like

Marianne's is what puts a lot of women off using the personal columns – and of course it is essential to take care, and trust your gut feelings. But, although meeting someone through an ad can be nerve-racking, it is no more so than meeting someone at a party. In some ways, it's actually preferable to be in control of the situation in this way, rather than be at the mercy of circumstances. After all, when you encounter someone at a party you can't tell straight away whether they're involved with anybody else (unless they're wearing a wedding ring, of course). Even if this proves not to be the case, you still have to decide whether you have anything in common, beyond mutual attraction. Whereas when you arrange to meet someone through an ad you are very much in the driving seat. *You* choose the person you want to meet. *You* decide how far things will progress. In the end, it's not so very different from the traditional 'blind date', whereby two people meet through shared friends, decide if they like each other and are attracted to each other, and discuss seeing each other again. Once the initial embarrassment is past ('Are you Miss X?' 'You must be Mr Y...') you can treat each other just like any other couple.

Online dating

A high-tech version of the traditional lonely-hearts method, finding a partner through the Internet has become wildly popular in recent years. It offers both the anonymity of the small ads and the opportunity to communicate at length with a prospective partner – without necessarily revealing anything about yourself. The online 'chat rooms' and dating services seem like the answer to a shy person's prayer. Unlike more old-fashioned methods of advertising for a partner – such as local or national newspapers – getting to know someone through the Internet can be instantaneous. It's also international – in the few seconds it takes to log on, you can be talking about classical music to a soulmate in Minnesota, or chatting up a glamorous-sounding lifeguard on Bondi Beach.

It can also feel quite liberating, pouring out your thoughts and dreams to total strangers, whom you're unlikely ever to meet in the flesh. (Although of course people do decide to meet – and successful relationships have started in this way. My sister, who lives in Canada, recently attended a wedding where bride and groom had met online.) But do be wary. Sometimes, the people you 'meet' on the Net are not all they claim to be. Recent cases in the national press have drawn attention to the dangers of online dating – especially where minors are concerned. Remember, you can't see the person you're 'talking' to and you can't hear their voice. They may be hiding behind not just a 'cyber-name' but a whole different identity. Blonde Bombshell from Beverly Hills may turn out in real life to be fat and forty. Hunky Hank from Huddersfield may not be the sexy 25-year-old he claims to be.

When contacting people online it helps to keep in mind the basic rules of common sense you'd apply to any unfamiliar situation. In other words, don't give out more about yourself than you'd be prepared to tell anyone you'd met for the first time.

Some Net do's and don'ts

- **Don't** tell someone your address or telephone number unless you're absolutely certain you want them to contact you this way. Many Internet 'romances' last for months before either of the participants divulges this kind of personal information.
- **Don't** be afraid to terminate the 'conversation' immediately, if you feel uncomfortable with something that's been said.
- **Don't** just focus your attention on dating websites: you're more likely to meet someone who shares your interests on one of the special-interest websites – for music or theatre, say – than by simply going for the obvious lonely-hearts connection.

- **Do** try to move the relationship offline as soon as possible. If someone is genuine (and genuinely likes the sound of you) they'll want to meet via the telephone, and – hopefully – face to face.
- **Do** tell your friends if you are going to meet someone you've encountered in this way. If the person is genuine, then they're not going to mind if you say you've taken this precaution. If they're married – or otherwise stringing you along – their reaction to the news may be all you need to know.
- **Do** enjoy your computer dating sessions. For shy people, especially, it's a wonderful opportunity to practise your flirting skills, in the privacy (and safety) of your own desktop area. And – despite the precautions advised above – romance *can* flourish in cyberspace. You just need to give it a chance!

Holidays

Going on holiday to some preferably exotic place is supposedly another sure-fire way of meeting the man (or woman) of your dreams. Hot climates make us all feel – and look – more sensual: we tend to wear fewer clothes, have more time on our hands for flirting, and generally feel more up for it where sex is concerned than when we're at home, caught up in our normal routines. But, while it's certainly true that romances can (and do) occur under such circumstances, it also should be borne in mind that most holiday flings are by definition short-lived. If that's what you're looking for, then fine. Just don't pin your hopes on finding a long-term love. That said, you shouldn't rule it out, either! One friend of mine, Kate, met the man who is now her husband when both were on a working holiday in the Seychelles (they are both travel journalists).

'We instantly clicked,' she recalls. 'I'd just broken up with

Mark, the man I'd been seeing for a couple of years, so I was up for a bit of fun, that's all. I liked Will a lot – he was so funny and attractive – but I remember thinking, Don't get too involved. He's bound to have a girlfriend back home – which in fact turned out to be the case.'

In spite of her misgivings, Kate found herself succumbing to the combined effects of sun, sea and Will's undivided attention, and, by the end of the week, they were definitely an item. 'We had a brilliant few days together, swimming, sunbathing and just talking, but I'd convinced myself that it wasn't going to last. I'd had friends who'd done just what I'd done – fallen for a bloke on holiday and then been let down. I was determined it wasn't going to happen to me, so I sort of kept Will a bit at arm's length, emotionally speaking. When we said goodbye at Heathrow I remember saying to myself, That's the last you'll see of *him*. I couldn't have been more surprised when, a week or so after we'd returned to London, Will rang me. He'd been thinking about me ever since we'd met, he said, and had decided he couldn't live without me! He and his then girlfriend had been on the verge of splitting up for some months, so I suppose meeting me was just the catalyst.'

Happy-ever-after experiences such as Kate's can happen, of course – but the reality is that most holiday affairs end when you step onto the flight back home, if not before. Another recently divorced friend, Caro, went to Spain with a girlfriend for a couple of weeks, where she met Jason, a handsome Australian several years younger than she was who had a summer job in one of the beachside cafés. 'Jason was great – a real Bondi Beach type, with a fantastic body and an all-over suntan. I was just so flattered that he seemed attracted to me, and not to some girl his own age. But he kept telling me I was the most fabulous woman there. It did wonders for my ego.'

After two weeks, Caro had to return home, but not before she and Jason had arranged for him to come and see her in London, when his seasonal job came to an end. 'For a while it was lovely,' Caro remembers. 'The café where Jason worked was one of those ones where you can send emails, so I used to get these silly, romantic messages flashing up on my computer all the time.' What happened afterwards was somewhat less romantic, however. Jason did indeed turn up in London – bringing a girlfriend with him. 'When he asked if they could sleep on the floor in my flat for a few days, I couldn't believe my ears,' laughs Caro ruefully. 'I think he was quite surprised when I refused.'

Disastrous stories aside (and everybody has at least *one*), going abroad as a single woman can do wonders for your confidence and – even though the likelihood of meeting Mr Right in the passport queue is slim – there are lots of other reasons for doing it. If you go with a group of – preferably single – friends, the opportunities for having fun are endless, and not necessarily of the drunken girls'-night-out-in-Benidorm variety, either. I remember one walking holiday near Toulouse with a group of girlfriends – all intent on enjoying the same mixture of excellent food and wine, good company and beautiful scenery – which was among the best holidays I've ever had.

Another trip, this time on my own, was to China, where I fulfilled the dream of a lifetime by visiting the Forbidden City, walking the Great Wall of China and eating Peking duck in Beijing's most famous restaurant – an itinerary I would have thought completely beyond my capabilities to organise, even a few years ago. Being on your own makes you more resourceful: if *you* don't do something, no one else is going to do it for you. You start to realise that some things – arranging a trip abroad, for example – just aren't as difficult as you'd imagined. You come back from some exotic trip, all glowing and golden and full of your adventures, and have the satisfaction of hearing one of your (married) friends say, 'Ooh, aren't you lucky, swanning off to all these interesting places?' And suddenly it hits you – you *love* being single.

Surviving in your new relationship

For anyone who has been through a divorce or separation, the prospect of forming a new relationship can be a daunting one, beset with fear of repeating the mistakes of the past. Although it can be a wonderful experience to meet someone new when you have been through the trauma of rejection and break-up, it can also be highly stressful! There are several reasons for this – which I'll look at in turn – but the main one is that your expectations will be higher. You will be older and more experienced at relationships, it is true, than when you were first married or became involved with your previous partner, but this does not necessarily mean that you will be emotionally stronger. In fact, the reverse is probably the case. Starting a new relationship can feel like a romantic whirl – 'like being sixteen all over again', as one friend put it – but in fact it is a much more serious romantic venture than those of your teenage years. Anyone who has been hurt is likely to be more vulnerable, emotionally, than someone younger and less experienced, who will have less invested in a new relationship. Most of us can remember the happy carelessness with which we fell in and out of love affairs during our teens and early twenties. When you've been through a serious relationship, followed by a break-up, it makes you less casual about such things.

'After my divorce, I was much more reluctant to get seriously involved with anyone again,' says Gemma. 'I'd felt so let down by Paul, and so betrayed by him, that it was as much as I could do to trust anyone ever again. For the first couple of years I didn't go out with anyone at all. I was happy just being with the children, who were still young enough to need me around a lot. Then, about two and a half years after we split, a friend said, "You really should get out more, you know." She suggested I should leave the kids with my parents and join her and her boyfriend, as well as a couple of other singles in our group, to go on a skiing holiday. I did and it was fun. On the flight home, I sat next to Henri, who was French and very charming. He'd also been through a divorce, and had grown-up children. We exchanged phone numbers, and a couple of weeks later, when he was in London on business, he rang me. It was great going out with someone again. You need to feel special to another person, I think. Being with Henri was very good for my confidence. But the relationship didn't last – mainly because I was so wary of commitment that I never let it get beyond the casual stage. Also living in different countries (Henri lives in Paris) meant it always stayed an occasional thing. When we broke up, Henri told me he'd wanted to take the relationship further – and would even have been prepared to come to London to live – but felt I wasn't "ready". Looking back, I think he was probably right.'

Gemma has since met someone else, who shares her love of music and travel, and feels she may now be ready to settle into a committed relationship. 'People don't realise how devastating it is when a marriage breaks up,' she says. 'It's not just a question of finding someone new. You have to deal with a whole lot of emotional stuff. Five years on, I feel ready to handle a serious involvement. And Jonathan has been very patient – he's never tried to rush me into something I'm not ready for.'

Other stresses, too, apart from the (entirely reasonable) fear of getting hurt, are experienced by many people in second-time-around relationships.

Financial worries

These could be brought about by the strains of trying to run two households. Many men in this position, who are paying maintenance to support one family while trying to consolidate a new relationship (which may or may not include having more children), find themselves under this kind of strain, caught between their ex, who may feel she is being treated ungenerously, and their new partner, who may feel she, too, is getting a raw deal financially. Similarly, women whose divorce settlement has left them with a reduced budget on which to run the household may find that there is less money for extras – including spending money on their appearance, something that most of us would agree was vital in the early stages of a romance!

'Helen, my ex-wife, was always complaining she was short of money,' says Rod, a university lecturer. 'We'd agreed what seemed like a fairly generous settlement for her and the kids, and at first she was fine about it. Things changed when I met Clara. Suddenly, I started getting all these furious phone calls, saying I'd missed her last month's payment, or the girls needed new coats, or something. She started accusing me of spending less on her and the kids than on my "fancy woman", as she put it. I think she just couldn't take the fact that I'd found somebody new. One thing she got really annoyed about was when Clara and I went to stay with some friends of mine in California for a couple of weeks. Helen said that, in all the years we'd been together, we'd never had such an "extravagant" holiday! The silly thing was, I was living in a bedsit at the time, and spending just about all my income on paying the mortgage on the house for Helen and the girls. I certainly wasn't enjoying an "extravagant" lifestyle – but I know Helen felt otherwise. It caused a lot of angst.'

Emotional problems

These could manifest themselves as guilt, uncertainty and anger. Unresolved feelings of resentment towards the previous partner can ruin a new relationship in its early stages. 'You're always talking about *her*!' or 'You've never got over your feelings for *him*' are all too common complaints. For some people, the anger they feel towards their ex can spill over into their emotional life to the extent that they may seem more preoccupied with their old relationship than with their new. Sometimes, your partner's feelings of guilt and resentment towards his or her former partner

can seem uncomfortably close to emotional obsession –
especially if you don't have an ex of your own to contend with.
It can often seem as if your partner is still tied up with his or her
previous relationship – a situation that can be all the more intense
if he/she has children.

'It used to drive me mad, the way he was always on the phone
to Kate,' recalls Ceris of the early days of her relationship with
Sean. 'They'd be having these arguments about money all the
time – at one point, she was even threatening not to let him see
Liam, his little boy, unless he upped her maintenance payments.
It was awful. He'd get so upset about the things she said that it
would take all evening for him to calm down. I used to feel so
angry with her – and with him, in a way. One time I even said to
him, "I think you're still in love with her" – and, when he told me
not to be so stupid, I burst into tears! I felt I couldn't compete.'

Problems with your new partner's children
These could happen especially if they perceive you as the 'guilty'
party in the break-up. Children may be feeling a complex mixture
of emotions – sadness at the break-up, guilt (many children
'blame' themselves for their parents' separation), resentment that
their mother/father seems to 'prefer' her/his new partner to them,
and confusion at what has gone wrong in their lives. All this will
take time and patience to sort out – not always easy with the
demands of working life and a new relationship to contend with!
If *both* of you have children from the previous relationship this,
too, can cause stress. Children dread any withdrawal of a parent's
love and, even if this is not in fact the case, it can often *seem* as
if an absent parent who has gone to live with another partner and
his/her children had transferred his/her affections to the 'new'
family. As Joanna Trollope has shown in her remarkable novel,
Other People's Children, being a step-parent is far from easy –
and can even cause a new relationship to come unstuck, as
loyalties are tested and emotional commitments undermined.

'When I first met Adrian's kids, I felt like the enemy,' laughs Shona, who works as a PR manager in publishing. 'They really were the classic, stroppy teenagers. I got the works. Liddy – that's the fifteen-year-old – hardly spoke to me at all for the first six months that I was living with Adrian. When the children came to stay with us at weekends, she used to march in and go straight upstairs to her room until suppertime. Or she'd wear her headphones all the time, as an excuse not to talk. Petra, the middle one, was horse mad – so at least we had that in common! I used to ride when I was a teenager, and I had all my scrapbooks left over from taking part in gymkhanas. When I gave them to her to look at, she was quite impressed, I could tell – only she couldn't show it in front of her sister! Casper, who was only ten at the time of the divorce, was much easier to deal with on the whole – although he still had his moments. I think Maggie, Adrian's ex, used to say things to the kids about me, because one time Cas turned to me out of the blue and said, "What's a slut?" I almost fell off my chair.'

Accommodation problems

Again, the demands of providing for two households can put a new relationship under serious strain. If you have moved out of the family home, you may find you can afford only fairly modest accommodation for you and your new partner – a situation that can grow worse if you and your partner decide to have more children. If you are the full-time parent, left to run the family home, you may find that household expenses absorb a large part of your income. You may even envy your ex his or her 'fresh start' in a new home! With only a finite amount of money and property to divide, many divorced couples do feel the pinch, when it comes to making a new life. Compared with the financial security you may have felt in the past, the future can often look worryingly insecure, as job opportunities diminish and financial commitments increase. This, too, can severely tax a new relationship.

'Sometimes I feel I inherited all Dan's problems, as well as all the good stuff,' says Marie. 'When we first started living together, he'd not long been divorced from Sue, and was living in a shoebox in Hackney. It didn't matter at first, because we were so bound up with each other and carried away by the romance of it all; but, when I got pregnant, everything changed. Suddenly I realised I wanted my own home – not just a temporary place. Dan and I are both commercial artists, so I was able to work right through the pregnancy, as it happened. But studio space became a problem, because the flat was too small for us both to spend all our time there. It caused a lot of rows, being stuck in a grim little studio flat barely big enough for one, when there were about to be three of us.

'Eventually we managed to find a place – the proverbial rundown cottage in the country – where I was happy to have Daisy. But I can remember how miserable I felt during those months. I used to get so mad with Dan when he complained about all the money he was giving Sue and their kids. I used to feel like screaming, "What about me and our baby?" You get very emotional when you're pregnant.'

The disapproval of others

People can be very judgmental when one or other of the partners starts a new relationship, either before or immediately after a divorce. Unlike first-time newlyweds, who tend to meet only with approving and supportive responses from other people, second-time-around couples can sometimes meet with negative reactions, which may be caused by envy ('Traded in the old model for a new one, eh?'), protectiveness towards the former spouse ('She was so lovely; I can't think why you ever left her...') or moral and religious disapproval.

'When I first had to meet Jack's friends, I was really dreading it,' recalls Aileen. 'I knew some of them had been very close to Rebecca, his ex, and would probably hate me. He's quite a bit older than I am, and we'd got involved while he was still married to Rebecca. I knew most of his friends would know this, because they'd have heard her side of the story first. Even though Jack was the one to make the first move when we got together, I expected to be blamed for the break-up. In the event, that's exactly what happened. Jack even had a row with his oldest friend from university about me. This friend – or ex-friend, rather – told Jack I was just "using" him to advance my own career (Jack and I work for the same merchant bank). He said he'd be surprised if it lasted a year. In fact, we've been together six years now. Needless to say, we didn't ask that particular friend to the wedding!'

Stresses such as these (and there are doubtless others) can break a new relationship in its early stages. Of course, they can also make it stronger, as both partners struggle to overcome what may seem like insurmountable adversities. You'll certainly discover whether your relationship is a lasting one!

So how can you survive all this hostility and stress? And are there any ways you can prevent a new relationship breaking down? Well, first, it makes sense to establish some ground rules. Protect yourself and your relationship. You deserve some lasting happiness.

- **Be strong and single-minded.** If the relationship is what you want, *go for it*, as the saying goes. Don't let guilt – your own or other people's – spoil what could be a wonderful adventure. No, you're not sixteen any longer, but you've got what sixteen-year-olds don't have, which is a wealth of experience. You know what you want from life – in love as in every other aspect. So take it – and be happy.
- **Take one problem at a time and deal with it.** If you feel overwhelmed with difficulties (financial problems, problems with children) don't try to solve them all at once. Take each as it comes – and work through it together. After all, 'a problem shared is a problem halved' – and there are now two of you to

share it. Supporting your partner through his/her difficulties will help to strengthen the relationship.

- **Support each other.** You're not alone any more. Both of you have someone else to turn to. Try to be honest with your new partner. Don't make the mistakes that damaged your past relationship. If you work through each stage together and get to know how the other person thinks and what they want from the relationship, you can avoid the heartache and breakdowns of communication that happened before.

- **Enjoy being with your new partner.** After all the grief and disappointment, you need some fun. Take time out to be with the new person in your life. Don't make the mistake of rushing straight into domesticity, if you can help it. Living together can be wonderful – but try to act like lovers, not as if you had been married for years! Go to Paris, go to New York – or spend the weekend going round your local art gallery. Invite your friends for a celebratory meal – or just spend some time 'chilling out' with the Sunday papers. Whatever your preferred method of having fun, remember, you've come through a lot to enjoy it.

12
A New Beginning

So, is there life after divorce? And can anything positive ever come out of so much grief and pain? Well, my answer to that would be a very guarded 'yes'. Yes, divorce and separation can be devastating; and no, it doesn't have to be the end of the world. In fact, it can often be the start of a whole new life – socially, professionally and of course romantically. And, while no one would choose to go through the experience if they could avoid it, it is certainly true that, for the majority of the people I spoke with in researching this book, life as a divorced or newly single person has its compensations – not least of which is the feeling that you are in charge of your life once again.

'I'm so much more my own woman since the divorce,' says Sarah. 'When I was married to Ian, I'd let him make all the big decisions – about moving house and the children's schooling and whether we could afford a holiday that year. Now I'm the one who has to cope. It's made me much more self-reliant. The other day, Ian and I were discussing our respective summer holiday arrangements regarding the children. A few years ago, I'd have said, "What are *your* plans?" and then fitted in my own time with the kids around Ian's. This time I got in first by saying, "This is what *I'm* doing. It would suit me for you to have the kids between this date and that." It was brilliant. I think Ian was quite taken aback.'

'I've certainly grown as a person since Rob and I split,' says Jane. 'I was quite unsure of myself when we met, and he's a very dominant, overbearing type. I realise now how much I deferred to him. When it came to arguing over the divorce settlement, I discovered I could stand up to him in a way I never had when we were first together. I'd tell myself I had to do it for Caitlin, our daughter – because, if I didn't insist on proper maintenance arrangements, she was the one who'd suffer in the end. It's amazing what a difference having a few good rows can make! I think Rob suddenly started seeing me as a force to be reckoned with. Plus I got myself a good lawyer! But I now feel, looking back, that the turning point was when I realised I was on my own. There was no one to fight my battles for me but *me*. It was quite scary at first – but later I got to like being the one in charge. The great thing is that now it's Rob who defers to me when it's a question of Caitlin's future.'

'If you'd asked me two years ago whether I'd ever be happy about being divorced, I'd have said, "Are you out of your mind?"' admits Kate. 'I went through so much at the time, what with keeping the company going and looking after Liam, that I got quite seriously depressed. Then, about eighteen months ago, something clicked. I thought, I'm single. I'm free. I'm feeling good about life. It was as if everything suddenly fell into place. I'd got my life back again.'

Kate's view is that it took a mixture of things – clinching a new contract for her company, the fact that Liam, now five, was starting full-time school, and the news that a friend was seriously ill with cancer that made her put things in perspective. 'Hearing about Lynsey's illness made me take a long, hard look at my own life, and see how much I had to be grateful for. I had my health, my lovely little boy, my nice house and my own business. I suddenly saw my life for what it was – pretty terrific.'

In the past few months, Kate and Sean, her ex-husband, have been on better terms. 'It seemed to both of us that we ought to make an effort for Liam's sake – because, whatever happened between us, Sean is still his dad. Now it's actually much better, because we can be friends, even though we no longer live together. Getting divorced was hard for us both – but it's made us grow up, in a sense. Two years ago I couldn't have had a conversation with Sean without slamming the phone down. Now we get on quite well.'

'I do feel a lot happier now than when I was going through the divorce,' says Louise. 'Both John and I have mellowed enough to admit there were faults on both sides. I think the really awful thing about the way our society looks at divorce is that it's seen as this terrible failure. You can't help feeling that you've let everybody down – your friends, your family – and that no one will ever love or trust you again, whereas in fact, the opposite is the case. I'm much more sensitive to other people's problems since I had my own difficulties with the marriage. I'm quite used to friends phoning me up and saying, "You're the only person I can tell about this..." So far from being alone and isolated, I've actually got far more friends than I've ever had in my life. When I met Dan, my current partner, he said he was quite worried that I wouldn't have time for him, what with all the girlie nights out and heart-to-hearts with old boyfriends I seemed to be having! One thing I think it's important to remember when you're going through a separation is not to lose your self-esteem. You're not alone in experiencing break-up. It's not your "fault" your relationship has come to an end. You *will* be happy again. You *will* find love. When things are bad, it's sometimes necessary to remind yourself of these truths.'

'It's only when you're through it and out the other side that you realise how awful it was,' recalls Alice. 'I think it was a good two years before I got my confidence back. From being quite a social animal, I'd make any excuse not to go out. Then, one day, a friend said to me, "You can't hide behind those children of yours for ever. Get a babysitter." She and I started going out a couple of evenings a week – to go to a film or have a drink. Before I knew it, I was actually having fun! I joined a choir (before I got married, I used to sing semiprofessionally) and met a whole new circle of people. We've been to Bavaria, to Verona, and, most recently, Rome, competing in international singing festivals. It's something I'd never have done if I'd still been married.'

'Having been through a divorce makes you more open to the possibilities of a new relationship,' says Emma. 'You know what you want. You don't waste time with people who aren't serious about you.' When Emma's own marriage ended, she remained on good terms with her ex – and his new girlfriend. 'People often seemed to think it was weird, that Martin and I still saw each other occasionally for a meal or a glass of wine. There was never anything sexual about it – at least on my side. But then, one day, Martin said to me, "You know, I think I've made a big mistake." I didn't even have to think. I just said, "I'm sorry, but I know I haven't. This is the right decision for me." It was very liberating.'

Now in a new relationship, Emma is convinced that, if divorce and separation are handled the right way, it can not only minimise the damage suffered by children and family, but can help former partners to 'move on'. 'When Martin told me he thought he'd made a mistake in moving out, he was really saying that he wasn't ready for the finality of our separation. He didn't want to give me up, but he didn't want to give up Lauren, his girlfriend, either. In telling him I'd made the break, I was letting him go, I suppose.'

After the divorce was finalised, Emma had a series of casual relationships, which ended after a few months. 'I wasn't looking to settle down, at that point. I think, unconsciously, I was only letting myself be attracted to men who weren't prepared to commit! It wasn't until I met Steve that I knew I'd found somebody different. Somebody worth being serious about.

'In our parents' day, divorce was something to be ashamed of,' Emma reflects. 'Now it's something a very high proportion of people – something like one in three couples – will experience at some time in their lives. I read somewhere the other day that seventy per cent of divorces are initiated by the woman – and that makes a lot of sense to me, because in some ways life's better than it's ever been for single women. I'm in a relationship now, but for several years after I split up with Martin, I was happy to be on my own. I had men who were interested during that time – but there wasn't the feeling that you had to settle down and make a home with someone. I'd already been there and done that! I suppose in a funny way you could say I quite enjoyed being a divorcee. It gave me a confidence I hadn't had before – the feeling that I'd lived a bit. It certainly didn't do me any harm with the opposite sex – quite the reverse! Some men like a woman who's lived a bit. There's not the stigma there used to be – the idea that you're some kind of "scarlet woman" if you're a divorcee. I think people are much more sympathetic to the idea that marriages don't always last than they used to be. In this respect, we're a more tolerant society.'

'I'm far better about saying what *I* want from life since I split up with Matt,' says Jen. 'I mean I was never the sort to let a man walk all over me, but I did have a tendency, when I was married, to let the Man of the Household make all the really hard, scary decisions, like whether it was the right time to apply for a mortgage or whatever. Being on my own these past couple of years has cured me of that. I run my own show, now – and woe betide any bloke who tries to tell me what to do!

'The great thing is, people pick up on your confidence. I'm not saying it's helped me get on in my job since then, but being your own person does give you an aura of being able to cope. I've certainly not been doing badly at work! And it gives you an edge in other situations, too. The other day I was having lunch in a restaurant with some friends, several of whom are men, and I grabbed the wine list without thinking and started to order. You should have seen the wine waiter's face! But I like that – not being intimidated in situations where previously I'd have let a man take the lead. If I ever do settle down with someone on a permanent basis, I'll make sure he respects me for myself, and doesn't expect me to be the "little woman".'

'I knew I was over Patrick a few months ago,' Wendy recalls, 'when I was chucking out some stuff and found an old sweater of his that had got overlooked when he picked up his things. Two years ago I'd have broken down. But, since the counselling, I'm much less emotional about it all. I just put it in the bin liner for Oxfam and got on with the job. It doesn't sound like a big thing – but for me it was a huge advance, realising you're no longer emotionally dependent on someone. It's liberating. The funny thing is that friends keep telling me how great I look and saying how relaxed I seem. It makes me realise how miserable and tense I must have been when I was going through the divorce. The great thing is, you can put it all behind you. I'm not the most resilient person in the world and yet even I've been able to "get a life" and start afresh.'

'Rachel and I get on much better since the divorce,' says Tim. 'Looking back, I can see it all started to fall apart a lot longer ago than either of us realised. The separation was just the breaking point. We'd had years of tensions and petty rows leading up to it, so that when it happened it was almost a relief. If we hadn't had the kids to think about, I think we'd probably have separated long ago. But, as it is, we'll always have Poppy and Jack in common. Rachel's a wonderful mother. And I've really admired the way she's taken hold of her life these past few years. Now she's with Adam, her new partner, she seems much more grounded and settled. She said much the same about *me* only the other day, when we met to go to Poppy's school speech day! And it's true that with Hannah, my girlfriend, I'm trying not to repeat the mistakes of the past.

'If going through a divorce has taught me anything, it's to be a lot less inflexible and selfish about what I expect from another person. I think with Rachel and I there were faults on both sides, but I don't feel as much to blame as I used to – even though it was me who broke up the marriage. Rachel said the other day she'd forgiven me for that a long time ago. Which only goes to show how well she's coped with the whole thing. If I have any regrets, it's that the children were exposed to so much unhappiness from both of us. Things are a lot better now, of course. But still, you wouldn't want to put your kids through that again.'

For my own part, I would agree that going through a divorce can make you stronger. It can teach you things about yourself that you never knew before. Any painful or difficult experience can have this effect, of course – although most people would probably prefer not to have to find this out at first hand! But there are compensations (it has to be said) for the sadness and feelings of failure and loss one inevitably feels at the ending of a marriage. One of these is that you really do learn how to stand on your own two feet. Until my divorce, I was always one of those people who preferred to let someone else (parents, friends, husband) make the decisions. Now I make my own decisions, whether large or small.

I'm fortunate in that I have a very good relationship with my former partner – something that has been, I feel, of enormous benefit in enabling our two children to come to terms with the separation. It hasn't always been easy, but – mainly because we wanted to minimise problems for the children – both my ex and I have worked hard to overcome the difficulties that led up to our decision to part. Now we're like very good friends – we talk on the phone most days, attend our children's school and university events together, and even go to the odd party or wedding of shared friends together! I get on well with my ex's new partner, as he does with mine. My children have regular contact with their grandparents (my former in-laws), and both families occasionally meet up for family events such as weddings. Yes, it would have been better if we hadn't had to divorce, but, given that we did, our relationship is as good as – if not better than – it's ever been.

So, yes, divorce can be hateful and bitter and traumatic, but it can also be achieved in a civilised and relatively stress-free way. It can be wounding and demeaning and hurtful, but it can also be a curiously empowering experience that leaves you feeling stronger and more in control of your life. Above all, it can make you more aware of how fragile relationships can be. It can make you more sensitive to other people, and more in touch with your own feelings and desires. If you've known what it's like to be unhappy, then you learn how much happiness is to be prized! No, of course I would rather not have gone through my divorce – but, having gone through it, I feel I've survived it pretty well.

Suggested Reading

Nonfiction

Breaking Up Without Cracking Up by Christopher Compston (HarperCollins, 1998).

Get Over It! by Sue Ostler (Allen & Unwin, 1998).

The Heart-Shaped Bullet by Kathryn Flett (Picador, 1999).

How to Do Your Own Divorce by Jeremy Rosenblatt (Vermilion, 1993).

How to Survive Divorce by Roy van der Brink-Budgen (How To Books, 1995).

Mars and Venus Starting Over by John Gray (Vermilion, 1998).

National Family Mediation Guide to Separation and Divorce by Thelma Fisher (Vermilion, 1997).

A Practical Guide to Legal Aid (Legal Aid Head Office, 6th floor 29–37 Red Lion St, London WC1R 4PP).

The Relate Guide to Starting Again by Sarah Litvinoff (Vermilion, 1993).

Single and Loving It by Wendy Bristow (Thorsons, 2000).

Surviving the Break-up: How parents and children cope with divorce by Judith Wallerstein and Joan Kelly (Grant McIntyre, 1980).

Uncoupling: How and Why Relationships Come Apart by Diane Vaughan (Methuen, 1987).

The Which? Guide to Divorce by Helen Garlick (Which? Books/Penguin 1996).

Fiction

Lessons for a Sunday Father by Claire Calman (Black Swan, 2001).
Marrying the Mistress by Joanna Trollope (Bloomsbury, 2000).
Other People's Children by Joanna Trollope (Bloomsbury, 1998).

Children's fiction

An Angel for May by Melvin Burgess (Puffin, 1992).
The Divorce Express by Paula Danziger (Mammoth, 1982).
Goggle-Eyes by Anne Fine (Penguin, 1989).
Madame Doubtfire by Anne Fine (Puffin, 1987).

Useful organisations

Association for Shared Parenting
PO Box 2000
Dudley
West Midlands DY1 1YZ
01384 455665
http://fp.sharedparenting.f9.co.uk

Both Parents Forever
39 Cloonmore Avenue
Orpington
Kent BR6 9LE
01689 854433
http://www.youthinformation.com

British Association of Lawyer Mediators
The Shooting Lodge
Guildford Rd
Guildford
Surrey GU4 7PZ
01483 235000
http://www.balm.org.uk

Cambridge Family and Divorce Centre
1 Brooklands Avenue
Cambridge CB2 2BB
01223 576308
http://www.directions-plus.org.uk/az/com_fam_divorce.cert.html

Child Abduction Unit
Official Solicitor's Dept
4th Floor
81 Chancery Lane
London WC2A 1DD
020 7911 7047/7094
http://www.offsol.demon.co.uk

Childline
0800 1111
http://www.childline.org.uk

The Child Poverty Action Group
1/5 Bath St
London EC1V 9PY
020 7253 3406
http://www.cpag.org.uk

Child Support Agency
PO Box 55
Brierley Hill
West Midlands DY5 1YL
0345 133133
http://www.csa.gov.uk

The Divorce Corporation
Monnybrook House
Moss Rd
Totely Bents
Sheffield
South Yorkshire S17 3BB
0114 262 0616
http://www.divorcepensionreports.co.uk

Divorce Mediation and Counselling Service
38 Ebury Street
London SW1W 0LU
020 7730 2422

Divorce Registry
Somerset House
The Strand
London WC2R 1LP

Families Need Fathers
134 Curtain Rd
London EC2A 3AR
020 7613 5060/020 8886 0970
http://www.fnf.co.uk

Family Law Consortium
2 Henrietta Street
London WC2E 8PS
020 7420 5000
http://tflc.co.uk/divorce.html

Family Mediation Scotland
127 Rose St
South Lane

Edinburgh EH2 4BB
0131 220 1610
http://www.familymediationscotland.org.uk

Family Mediation Service
76 Dublin Road
Belfast BT2 7HP
01232 322914

Family Mediators Association
PO Box 2028
Hove
East Sussex BN3 3HU
01273 747750

Family Welfare Association
501–505 Kingsland Rd
London E8 4AU
020 7254 6251
http://www.charitiesdirect.com

Gingerbread
16–17 Clerkenwell Close
London EC1R 0AA
020 7336 8184
http://www.gingerbread.co.uk

Law Society of England and Wales
Ince House
60 Kenilworth Rd
Leamington Spa
Warwickshire CV32 6JY
01926 886990
http://www.lawsoc.org.uk

Law Society of Northern Ireland
Law Society House
98 Victoria St
Belfast BT1 3JZ
01232 231614
http://www.nilad.org.uk

Law Society of Scotland
26 Drumsheugh Gardens
Edinburgh EH3 7YR
0131 226 7411
http://www.lawsoc.org.uk

Legal Aid Board
85 Grays Inn Rd
London WC1X 8AA
020 7813 1000
http://www.legalservices.gov.uk

London Women's Aid
PO Box 14041
London E1 6NY
020 7392 2092
National helpline: 0345 023468
http://www.womeninlondon.gn.apc.org

National Council for the Divorced and Separated
PO Box 519
Leicester
Leicestershire LE2 3ZE
National helpline: 0116 270 0595
http://www.ncdsni.co.uk

National Council for One-Parent Families
255 Kentish Town Rd
London NW5 2LX
020 7267 1361
http://www.ncopt.org.uk

National Family Mediation
9 Tavistock Place
London WC1H 9SN
020 7383 5993
http://www.nfm.u-net.com

National Stepfamily Association
Chapel House
18 Hatton Place
London EC1N 8RU
020 7209 2460

Office for the Supervision of Solicitors
Victoria Court
8 Dormer Place
Leamington Spa
Warwickshire CV32 5AE
01926 822007/8/9

Relate – National Marriage Guidance Council
Herbert Gray College
Little Church St
Rugby
Warwickshire CV21 3AP
01788 573241
http://www.relate.org.uk

Solicitors Family Law Association
PO Box 302
Orpington
Kent BR6 8QX
01689 850227
http://www.sfla.co.uk

Women's Aid Federation
PO Box 391
Bristol BS99 7WS
0345 023468
http://www.womensaid.org.uk